The Duke of Milan by Philip Massinger

Philip Massinger was baptized at St. Thomas's in Salisbury on November 24th, 1583.

Massinger is described in his matriculation entry at St. Alban Hall, Oxford (1602), as the son of a gentleman. His father, who had also been educated there, was a member of parliament, and attached to the household of Henry Herbert, 2nd Earl of Pembroke. The Earl was later seen as a potential patron for Massinger.

He left Oxford in 1606 without a degree. His father had died in 1603, and accounts suggest that Massinger was left with no financial support this, together with rumours that he had converted to Catholicism, meant the next stage of his career needed to provide an income.

Massinger went to London to make his living as a dramatist, but he is only recorded as author some fifteen years later, when The Virgin Martyr (1621) is given as the work of Massinger and Thomas Dekker.

During those early years as a playwright he wrote for the Elizabethan stage entrepreneur, Philip Henslowe. It was a difficult existence. Poverty was always close and there was constant pleading for advance payments on forthcoming works merely to survive.

After Henslowe died in 1616 Massinger and John Fletcher began to write primarily for the King's Men and Massinger would write regularly for them until his death.

The tone of the dedications in later plays suggests evidence of his continued poverty. In the preface of The Maid of Honour (1632) he wrote, addressing Sir Francis Foljambe and Sir Thomas Bland: "I had not to this time subsisted, but that I was supported by your frequent courtesies and favours."

The prologue to The Guardian (1633) refers to two unsuccessful plays and two years of silence, when the author feared he had lost popular favour although, from the little evidence that survives, it also seems he had involved some of his plays with political characters which would have cast shadows upon England's alliances.

Philip Massinger died suddenly at his house near the Globe Theatre on March 17th, 1640. He was buried the next day in the churchyard of St. Saviour's, Southwark, on March 18th, 1640. In the entry in the parish register he is described as a "stranger," which, however, implies nothing more than that he belonged to another parish.

Index of Contents

DRAMATIS PERSONSAE
Ludovico Sforza, supposed duke of Milan.
Francisco, his especial favourite.
Tiberio   }
Stephano   } Lords of his council
Graccho, a creature of Mariana.
Julio   }
Giovanni   } Courtiers
Charles, the Emperor.
Pescara, an imperialist, but a friend to Sforza.
Hernando   }
Medina   } Captains to the Emperor.
Alphonso   }
Three Gentlemen.
Fiddlers.
An Officer.
Two Doctors.
Two Couriers.
Marcelia, the dutchess, wife to Sforza.
Isabella, mother to Sforza.
Mariana, wife to Francisco, and siste.
Sforza.
Eugenia, sister to Francisco.
A Gentlewoman.
Guards, Servants, Attendants.

SCENE: For the first and second acts, in Milan; during part of the third, in the Imperial Camp near Pavia; the rest of the play, in Milan, and its neighbourhood.

ACT I

SCENE I. Milan. An Outer Room in the Castle

Enter **GRACCHO**, **JULIO**, and **GIOVSANNI**, with Flaggons.

GRACCHO
Take every man his flaggon: give the oath
To all you meet; I am this day the state drunkard,
I am sure against my will; and if you find
A man at ten that's sober, he's a traitor,
And, in my name, arrest him.

JULIO
Very good, sir:
But, say he be a sexton?

GRACCHO
If the bells
Ring out of tune, as if the street were burning,
And he cry, 'Tis rare music! bid him sleep:
'Tis a sign he has ta'en his liquor; and if you meet
An officer preaching of sobriety,
Unless he read it in Geneva print,
Lay him by the heels.

JULIO
But think you 'tis a fault
To be found sober?

GRACCHO
It is capital treason:
Or, if you mitigate it, let such pay
Forty crowns to the poor: but give a pension
To all the magistrates you find singing catches,
Or their wives dancing; for the courtiers reeling,
And the duke himself, I dare not say distemper'd,
But kind, and in his tottering chair carousing,
They do the country service, If you meet
One that eats bread, a child of ignorance,
And bred up in the darkness of no drinking,
Against his will you may initiate him
In the true posture; though he die in the taking

His drench, it skills not: what's a private man,
For the public honour! We've nought else to think on.
And so, dear friends, copartners in my travails,
Drink hard; and let the health run through the city,
Until it reel again, and with me cry,
Long live the dutchess!

[Enter **TIBERIO** and **STEPHANO**.

JULIO
I. Here are two lords; what think you?
Shall we give the oath to them?

GRACCHO
Fie! no: I know them,
You need not swear them; your lord, by his patent,
Stands bound to take his rouse. Long live the dutchess!

[Exeunt **GRACCHO, JULIO** and **GIOVANNI**.

STEPHANO
The cause of this? but yesterday the court
Wore the sad livery of distrust and fear;
No smile, not in a buffoon to be seen,
Or common jester: the Great Duke himself
Had sorrow in his face! which, waited on
By his mother, sister, and his fairest dutchess,
Dispersed a silent mourning through all Milan;
As if some great blow had been given the state,
Or were at least expected.

TIBERIO
Stephano,
I know as you are noble, you are honest,
And capable of secrets of more weight
Than now I shall deliver. If that Sforza,
The present duke, (though his whole life hath been
But one continued pilgrimage through dangers,
Affrights, and horrors, which his fortune, guided
By his strong judgment, still hath overcome,)
Appears now shaken, it deserves no wonder:
All that his youth hath labour'd for, the harvest
Sown by his industry ready to be reap'd too,
Being now at stake; and all his hopes confirm'd,
Or lost for ever.

STEPHANO
I know no such hazard:

His guards are strong and sure, his coffers full;
The people well affected; and so wisely
His provident care hath wrought, that though war rages
In most parts of our western world, there is
No enemy near us.

TIBERIO
Dangers, that we see
To threaten ruin, are with ease prevented;
But those strike deadly, that come unexpected:
The lightning is far off, yet, soon as seen,
We may behold the terrible effects
That it produceth. But I'll help your knowledge,
And make his cause of fear familiar to you.
The wars so long continued between
The emperor Charles, and Francis the
French king,
Have interess'd, in cither's cause, the most
Of the Italian princes; among which, Sforza,
As one of greatest power, was sought by both;
But with assurance, having one his friend,
The other lived his enemy.

STEPHANO
'Tis true:
And 'twas a doubtful choice.

TIBERIO
But he, well knowing,
And hating too, it seems, the Spanish pride,
Lent his assistance to the king of France:
Which hath so far incensed the emperor,
That all his hopes and honours are embark'd
With his great patron's fortune.

STEPHANO
Which stands fair,
For aught I yet can hear.

TIBERIO
But should it change,
The duke's undone. They have drawn to the field
Two royal armies, full of fiery youth;
Of equal spirit to dare, and power to do:
So near intrench 'd, that 'tis beyond all hope
Of human counsel they can e'er be severed,
Until it be determined by the sword,
Who hath the better cause: for the. success,

Concludes the victor innocent, and the vanquish 'd
Most miserably guilty, j How uncertain
The fortune of the war is, children know;
And, it being in suspense, on whose fair tent
Wing'd Victory will make her glorious stand,
You cannot blame the duke, though he appear
Perplex 'd and troubled.

STEPHANO
But why, then,
In such a time, when every knee should bend
For the success and safety of his person,
Are these loud triumphs? In my weak opinion,
They are unseasonable.

TIBERIO
I judge so too;
But only in the cause to be excused.
It is the dutchess' birthday, once a year
Solemnized with all pomp and ceremony;
In which the duke is not his own, but hers:
Nay, every day, indeed, he is her creature,
For never man so doated; but to tell
The tenth part of his fondness to a stranger^
Would argue me of fiction.

STEPHANO
She's, indeed,
A lady of most exquisite form.

TIBERIO
She knows it,
Arid how to prize it.

STEPHANO
I ne'er heard her tainted
In any point of honour.

TIBERIO
On my life,
She's constant to his bed, and well deserves
His largest favours. But, when beauty is
Stamp'd on great women, great in birth and fortune,
And blown by flatterers greater than it is
Tis seldom unaccompanied with pride;
Nor is she that way free: presuming on
The duke's affection, and her own desert,
She bears herself with such a majesty,

Looking with scorn on all as things beneath her,
That Sforza's mother, that would lose no part
Of what was once her own, nor his fair sister,
A lady too acquainted with her worth,
Will brook it well; and howsoe'er their hate
Is smother'd tor a time, 'tis more than fear'd
It will at length break out.

STEPHANO
He in whose power it is,
Turn all to the best!

TIBERIO
Come, let us to the court;
We there shall see all bravery and cost,
That art can boast of.

STEPHANO
I'll bear you company.

[Exeunt.

SCENE II. Another Room in the Same

Enter **FRANCISCO**, **ISABELLA**, and **MARIANA**.

MARIANA
I will not go; I scorn to be a spot
In her proud train.

ISABELLA
Shall I, that am his mother,
Be so indulgent, as to wait on her
That owes me duty?

FRANCISCO
'Tis done to the duke,
And not to her: and, my sweet wife, remember,
And, madam, if you please, receive my counsel,
As Sforza is your son, you may command him;
And, as a sister, you may challenge from him
A brother's love and favour: but, this granted,
Consider he's the prince, and you his subjects,
And not to question or contend with her
Whom he is pleased to honour. Private men
Prefer their wives; and shall he, being a prince,

And blest with one that is the paradise
Of sweetness and of beauty, to whose charge
The stock of women's goodness is given up,
Not use her like herself?

ISABELLA
You are ever forward
To sing her praises.

MARIANA
Others are as fair;
I am sure, as noble.

FRANCISCO
I detract from none,
In giving her what's due. Were she deform'd,
Yet being the dutchess, I stand bound to serve her;
But, as she is, to admire her. Never wife
Met with a purer heat her husband's fervour;
A happy pair, one in the other blest!
She confident in herself he's wholly hers,
And cannot seek for change; and he secure,
That 'tis not in the power of man to tempt her.
And therefore to contest with her, that is
The stronger and the better part of him,
Is more than folly: you know him of a nature
Not to be played with; and, should you forget
To obey him as your prince, he'll not remember
The duty that he owes you.

ISABELLA
'Tis but truth:
Come, clear our brows, and let us to the banquet;
But not to serve his idol.

MARIANA
I shall do
What may become the sister of a prince;
But will not stoop beneath it.

FRANCISCO
Yet, be wise;
Soar not too high, to fall; but stoop to rise.

[Exeunt.

Enter **THREE GENTLEMEN**, setting forth a banquet.

1ST GENTLEMAN
Quick, quick, for love's sake! let the court put on
Her choicest outside: cost and bravery
Be only thought of.

2ND GENTLEMAN
All that may be had
To please the eye, the ear, taste, touch, or smell,
Are carefully provided.

3RD GENTLEMAN
There's a masque:
Have you heard what's the invention?

1ST GENTLEMAN
No matter:
It is intended for the dutchess' honour;
And if it give her glorious attributes,
As the most fair, most virtuous, and the rest,
'Twill please the duke

[Loud music.

They come.

3RD GENTLEMAN
All is in order.

[Flourish. Enter **TIBERIO, STEPHANO, FRANCISCO, SFORZA, MARCELIA, ISABELLA, MARIANA,** and **ATTENDANTS**.

SFORZA
You are the mistress of the feast sit here,
O my soul's comfort! and when Sforza bows
Thus low to do you honour, let none think
The meanest service they can pay my love,
But as a fair addition to those titles
They stand possest of. Let me glory in
My happiness, and mighty kings look pale
With envy, while I triumph in mine own.
O mother, look on her! sister, admire her!
And, since this present age yields not a woman
Worthy to be her second, borrow of
Times past, and let imagination help,

Of those canonized ladies Sparta boasts of,
And, in her greatness, Rome was proud to owe,
To fashion one; yet still you must confess,
The phoenix of perfection ne'er was seen,
But in my fair Marcelia.

FRANCISCO
She 's, indeed,
The wonder oi all times.

TIBERIO
Your excellence,
Though I confess, you give her but her own,
Forces her modesty to the defence
Of a sweet blush.

SFORZA
It need not, my Marcelia;
When most I strive to praise thee, I appear
A poor detractor: for thou art, indeed,
So absolute in body and in mind,
That, but to speak the least part to the height,
Would ask an angel's tongue, and yet then end
In silent admiration!

ISABELLA
You still court her,
As if she were a mistress, not your wife.

SFORZA
A mistress, mother! she is more to me,
And every day deserves more to be sued to.
Such as are cloy'd with those they have embraced,
May think their wooing done: no night to me
But is a bridal one, where Hymen lights
His torches fresh and new; and those delights,
Which are not to be clothed in airy sounds,
Enjoy 'd, beget desires as full of heat,
And jovial fervour, as when first I tasted
Her virgin fruit. Blest night! and be it number'd
Amongst those happy ones, in which a blessing
Was, by the full consent of all the stars,
Conferr'd upon mankind.

MARCELIA
My worthiest lord!
The only object I behold with pleasure,
My pride, my glory, in a word, my all!

Bear witness, heaven, that I esteem myself
In nothing worthy of the meanest praise
You can bestow, unless it be in this,
That in my heart I love and honour you.
And, but that it would smell of arrogance,
To speak my strong desire and zeal to serve you,
I then could say, these eyes yet never saw
The rising sun, but that my vows and prayers
Were sent to heaven for the prosperity
And safety of my lord: nor have I ever
Had other study, but how to appear
Worthy your favour; and that my embraces
Might yield a fruitful harvest of content
For all your noble travail, in the purchase
Of her that's still your servant: By these lips,
Which, pardon me, that I presume to kiss

SFORZA
O swear, for ever swear!

MARCELIA
I ne'er will seek
Delight but in your pleasure: and desire,
When you are sated with all earthly glories,
And age and honours make you fit for heaven,
That one grave may receive us.

SFORZA
Tis believed,
Believed, my blest one.

MARIANA
How she winds herself
Into his soul!

SFORZA
Sit all. Let others feed
On those gross cates, while Sforza banquets with
Immortal viands ta'en in at his
I could live ever thus. Command the eunuch
To sing the ditty that I last composed, a f.

[Enter a **COURIER**.

In praise of my Marcelia. From whence?

COURIER
From Pavia, my dread lord.

SFORZA
Speak, is all lost?

COURIER [Delivers a letter]
The letter will inform you.

[Exit.

FRANCISCO
How his hand shakes,
As he receives it!

MARIANA
This is some allay
To his hot passion.

SFORZA
Though it bring death, I'll read it:
May it please your excellence to understand, that the very hour I wrote this, I heard a bold defiance delivered by a herald from the emperor, which was cheerfully received by the king of France. The battailes being ready to join, and the vanguard committed to my charge, enforces me to end, abruptly.
Your Highness' s humble servant.

GASPERO
Ready to join! By this, then, I am nothing.
Or my estate secure. [Aside.

MARCELIA
My lord.

SFORZA
To doubt,
Is worse than to have lost; and to despair,
Is but to antedate those miseries
That must fall on us; all my hopes depending
Upon this battle's fortune. In my soul,
Methinks, there should be that imperious power,
By supernatural, not usual means,
T' inform me what I am. The cause consider'd,
Why should I fear? The French are bold and strong,
Their numbers full, and in their councils wise;
But then, the haughty Spaniard is all fire,
Hot in his executions; fortunate
In his attempts; married to victory:
Ay, there it is that shakes me. [Aside.

FRANCISCO
Excellent lady,
This day was dedicated to your honour;
One gale of your sweet breath will easily
Disperse these clouds; and, but yourself, there's none
That dare speak to him.

MARCELIA
I will run the hazard!
My lord!

SFORZA
Ha! pardon me, Marcelia, I am troubled;
Arid stand uncertain, whether I am master
Of aught that's worth the owning.

MARCELIA
I am yours, sir;
And I have heard you swear, I being safe,
There was no loss could move you. This day, sir,
Is by your gift made mine. Can you revoke
A grant made to Marcelia? your Marcelia?
For whose love, nay, whose honour, gentle sir,
All deep designs, and state-affairs deferr'd,
Be, as you purposed, merry.

SFORZA
Out of my sight!

[Throws away the letter.

And all thoughts that may strangle mirth forsake me.
Fall what can fall, I dare the worst of fate:
Though the foundation of the earth should shrink,
The glorious eye of heaven lose his splendour,
Supported thus, I'll stand upon the ruins,
And seek for new life here. Why are you sad?
No other sports! by heaven, he's not my friend,
That wears one furrow in his face, I was told there was a masque.

FRANCISCO
They wait your highness' pleasure,
And when you please to have it.

SFORZA
Bid them enter:
'ome, make me happy once again. I am rapt
'Tis not to-day, to-morrow, or the next,

But all my days, and years, shall be eniploy'd
To do thee honour.

MARCELIA
And my life to serve you.

[A horn without.

SFORZA
Another post! Go hang him, hang him, I say;
I will not interrupt my present pleasures,
Although his message should import my head:
Hang him, I say.

MARCELIA
Nay, good sir, I am pleased
To grant a little intermission to you;
Who knows but he brings news we wish to hear,
To heighten our delights.

SFORZA
As wise as fair!

[Enter another **COURIER**.

From Gaspero?

COURIER
That was, my lord,

SFORZA
How! dead?

COURIER [Delivers a letter]
With the delivery of this, and prayers,
To guard your excellency from certain dangers,
He ceased to be a man.

[Exit.

SFORZA
All that my fears
Could fashion to me, or my enemies wish,
Is fallen upon me. Silence that harsh music;
'Tis now unseasonable: a tolling bell,
As a sad harbinger to tell me, that
This pamper'd lump of flesh must feast the worms,
Is fitter for me: I am sick.

MARCELIA
My lord!

SFORZA
Sick to the death, Marcelia. Remove
These signs of mirth; they were ominous, and but usher' d
Sorrow and ruin.

MARCELIA
Bless us, heaven!

ISABELLA
My son.

MARCELIA
What sudden change is this?

SFORZA
All leave the room;
I'll bear alone the burden of my grief,
And must admit no partner. I am yet
Your prince, where's your obedience? Stay,
Marcelia;
I cannot be so greedy of a sorrow,
In which you must not share.

[Exeunt **TIBERIO, STEPHANO, FRANCISCO, ISABELLA, MARIANA,** and **ATTENDANTS.**

MARCELIA
And cheerfully
I will sustain my part. Why look you pale?
Where is that wonted constancy and courage,
That dared the worst of fortune? where is Sforza,
To whom all dangers that fright common men,
Appear'd but panic terrors? why do you eye me
With such fix'd looks? Love, counsel, duty, service,
May flow from me, not danger.

SFORZA
O, Marcelia!
It is for thee I fear; for thee, thy Sforza
Shakes like a coward: for myself, unmoved,
I could have heard my troops were cut in pieces,
My general slain, and he, on whom my hopes
Of rule, of state, of life, had their dependence,
The king of France, my greatest friend, made prisoner
To so proud enemies.

MARCELIA
Then you have just cause
To shew you are a man.

SFORZA
All this were nothing,
Though I add to it, that I am assured,
For giving aid to this unfortunate king,
The emperor, incens'd, lays his command
On his victorious army, flesh'd with spoil,
And bold of conquest, to march up against me,
And seize on my estates: suppose that done too,
The city ta'en, the kennels running blood,
The ransack'd temples falling on their saints:
My mother, in my sight, toss'd on their pikes,
And sister ravish 'd; and myself bound fast
In chains, to grace their triumph; or what else
An enemy's insolence could load me with,
I would be Sforza still. But, when I think
That my Marcelia, to whom all these
Are but as atoms to the greatest hill,
Must suffer in my cause, and for me suffer!
All earthly torments, nay, even those the damn'd
Howl for in hell, are gentle strokes, compared
To what I feel, Marcelia.

'MARCELIA
Good sir, have patience:
I can as well partake your adverse fortune,
As I thus long have had an ample share
In your prosperity. 'Tis not in the power
Of fate to alter me; for while I am,
In spite of it, I'm yours.

SFORZA
But should that will
To be so [be] forced, Marcelia; and I live
To see those eyes I prize above my own,
Dart favours, though compell'd, upon another;
Or those sweet lips, yielding immortal nectar,
Be gently touch'd by any but myself;
Think, think, Marcelia, 'what a cursed thing
I were, beyond expression!

MARCELIA
Do not feed
Those jealous thoughts; the only blessing that

Heaven hath bestow'd on us, more than on beasts,
Is, that 'tis in our pleasure when to die.
Besides, were I now in another's power,
There are so many ways to let out life,
I would not live, for one short minute, his;
I was born only yours, and I will die so.

SFORZA
Angels reward the goodness of this woman!

[Enter **FRANCISCO**.

All I can pay is nothing. Why, uncall'd for?

FRANCISCO
It is of weight, sir, that makes me thus press
Upon your privacies. Your constant friend,
The marquis of Pescara, tired with haste.
Hath business that concerns your life and fortunes,
And with speed, to impart.

SFORZA
Wait on him hither.

[Exit **FRANCISCO**.

And, dearest, to thy closet. Let thy prayers
Assist my councils.

MARCELIA
To spare imprecations
Against myself, without you I am, nothing.

[Exit.

SFORZA
The marquis of Pescara! a great soldier;
And, though he serv'd upon the adverse party,
Ever my constant friend.

[Re-enter **FRANCISCO** with **PESCARA**.

FRANCISCO
Yonder he walks,
Full of sad thoughts.

PESCARA
Blame him not, good Francisco,

He hath much cause to grieve; would I might end so,
And not add this, to fear!

SFORZA
My dear Pescara;
A miracle in these times! a friend, and happy,
Cleaves to a falling fortune!

PESCARA
If it were
As well in my weak power, in act, to raise it,
As 'tis to bear a part of sorrow with you,
You then should have just cause to say,
Pescara
Look'd not upon your state, but on your virtues,
When he made suit to be writ in the list
Of those you favour'd. But my haste forbids
All compliment; thus, then, sir, to the purpose:
The cause that, unattended, brought me hither,
Was not to tell you of your loss, or danger;
For fame hath many wings to bring ill tidings,
And I presume you've heard it; but to give you
Such friendly counsel, as, perhaps, may make
Your sad disaster less.

SFORZA
You are all goodness;
And I give up myself to be disposed of,
As in your wisdom you think fit.

PESCARA
Thus, then, sir:
To hope you can hold out against the emperor,
Were flattery in yourself, to your undoing:
Therefore, the safest course that you can take,
Is, to give up yourself to his discretion,
Before you be compell'd; for, rest assured,
A voluntary yielding may find grace,
And will admit defence, at least, excuse:
But, should you linger doubtful, till his powers
Have seized your person and estates perforce,
You must expect extremes.

SFORZA
I understand you;
And I will put your counsel into act,
And speedily. I only will take order
For some domestical affairs, that do

Concern me nearly, and with the next sun
Ride with you: in the mean time, my best friend,
Pray take your rest.

PESCARA
Indeed, I have travell'd hard;
And will embrace your counsel.

[Exit.

SFORZA
With all care,
Attend my noble friend. Stay you, Francisco.
You see how things stand with me?

FRANCISCO
To my grief:
And if the loss of my poor life could be
A sacrifice to restore them as they were,
I willingly would lay it down.

SFORZA
I think so;
For I have ever found you true and thankful,
Which makes me love the building I have raised
In your advancement; and repent no grace
I have conferr'd upon you. And, believe me,
Though now I should repeat my favours to you,
The titles I have given you, and the means
Suitable to your honours; that I thought you
Worthy my sister and my family,
And in my dukedom made you next myself;
It is not to upbraid you; but to tell you
I find you are worthy of them, in your love
And service to me.

FRANCISCO
Sir, I am your creature;
And any shape, that you would have me wear,
I gladly will put on.

SFORZA
Thus, then, Francisco:
I now am to deliver to your trust
A weighty secret; of so strange a nature,
And 'twill, I know, appear so monstrous to you,
That you will tremble in the execution,
As much as I am tortured to command it:

For 'tis a deed so horrid, that, but to hear it,
Would strike into a ruffian flesh'd in murders,
Or an obdurate hangman, soft compassion;
And yet, Francisco, of all men the dearest,
And from me most deserving, such my state
And strange condition is, that thou alone
Must know the fatal service, and perform it.

FRANCISCO
These preparations, sir, to work a stranger,
Or to one unacquainted with your bounties.
Might appear useful; but to me they are
Needless impertinencies: for I dare do
Whate'er you dare command.

SFORZA
But you must swear it;
And put into the oath all joys or torments
That fright the wicked, or confirm the good;
Not to conceal it only, that is nothing,
But, whensoe'er my will shall speak, Strike now!
To fall upon't like thunder.

FRANCISCO
Minister
The oath in any way or form you please,
I stand resolved to take it.

SFORZA
Thou must do, then,
What no malevolent star will dare to look on,
It is so wicked: for which men will curse thee
For being the instrument; and the blest angels
Forsake me at my need, for being the author:
For 'tis a deed of night, of night, Francisco!
In which the memory of all good actions
We can pretend to, shall be buried quick:
Or, if we be remember'd, it shall be
To right posterity by our example,
That have out gone all precedents of villains
That were before us; and such as succeed.
Though taught in hell's black school, shall ne'er come near us.
Art thou not shaken yet?

FRANCISCO
I grant you move me:
But to a man confirm'd

SFORZA
I'll try your temper:
What think you of my wife?

FRANCISCO
As a thing sacred;
To whose fair name and memory I pay gladly
These signs of duty.

SFORZA
Is she not the abstract
Of all that's rare, or to be wish'd in woman?

FRANCISCO
It were a kind of blasphemy to dispute it:
But to the purpose, sir.

SFORZA
Add too, her goodness,
Her tenderness of me, her care to please me.
Her unsuspected chastity, ne'er equal! 'd;
Her innocence, her honour: O, I am lost
In the ocean of her virtues and her graces.
When I think of them!

FRANCISCO
Now I find the end
Of all your conjurations; there's some service
To be done for this sweet lady. If she have enemies,
That she would have removed

SFORZA
Alas! Francisco,
Her greatest enemy is her greatest lover;
Yet, in that hatred, her idolater.
One smile of hers would make a savage tame;
One accent of that tongue would calm the seas,
Though all the winds at once strove there for empire.
Yet I, for whom she thinks all this too little,
Should I miscarry in this present journey,
From whence it is all number to a cipher,
I ne'er return with honour, by thy hand
Must have her murder'd.

FRANCISCO
Murder'd! She that loves so,
And so deserves to be beloved again!
And I, who sometimes you were pleased to favour,

Pick'd out the instrument!

SFORZA
Do not fly off:
What is decreed can never be recall'd;
'Tis more than love to her, that marks her out
A wish'd companion to me in both fortunes:
And strong assurance of thy zealous faith,
That gives up to thy trust a secret, that
Racks should not have forced from me. O,
Francisco!

There is no heaven without her; nor a hell,
Where she resides. I ask from her but justice.
And what I would have paid to her, had sickness,
Or any other accident, divorced
Her purer soul from her unspotted body.
The slavish Indian princes, when they die,
Are cheerfully attended to the fire,
By the wife and slave that, living, they loved best,
To do them service in another world:
Nor will I be less honour'd, that love more.
And therefore trifle not, but, in thy looks,
Express a ready purpose to perform
What I command; or, by Marcelia's soul,
This is thy latest minute.

FRANCISCO
'Tis not fear
Of death, but love to you, makes me embrace it;
But for mine own security, when 'tis done,
What warrant have I? If you please to sign one,
I shall, though with unwillingness and horror,
Perform your dreadful charge.

SFORZA
I will, Francisco:
But still remember, that a prince's secrets
Are balm conceal'd; but poison, if discover'd.
I may come back; then this is but a trial
To purchase thee, if it were possible,
A nearer place in my affection: but
I know thee honest.

FRANCISCO
'Tis a character
I will not part with.

SFORZA
I may live to reward it.

[Exeunt.

ACT II

SCENE I. The Same. An Open Space Before the Castle

Enter **TIBERIO** and **STEPHANO**.

STEPHANO
How! left the court?

TIBERIO
Without guard or retinue
Fitting a prince.

STEPHANO
No enemy near, to force him
To leave his own strengths, yet deliver up
Himself, as 'twere, in bonds, to the discretion
Of him that hates him! 'tis beyond example.
You never heard the motives that induced him
To this strange course?

TIBERIO
No, those are cabinet councils,
And not to be communicated, but
To such as are his own, and sure. Alas!
We fill up empty places, and in public
Are taught to give our suffrages to that
Which was before determined; and are safe so.
Signior Francisco (upon whom alone
His absolute power is, with all strength, conferr'd,
During his absence) can with ease resolve you:
To me they are riddles.

STEPHANO
Well, he shall not be
My Œdipus; I'll rather dwell in darkness^
But, my good lord Tiberio, this Francisco
Is, on the sudden, strangely raised.

TIBERIO
O sir,

He took the thriving course; he had a sister,
A fair one too, with whom, as it is rumour 'd,
The duke was too familiar; but she, cast oft,
(What promises so ever past between them,)
Upon the sight of this, forsook the court,
And since was never seen. To smother this,
As honours never fail to purchase silence,
Francisco first was graced, and, step by step,
Is raised up to this height.

STEPHANO
But how is
His absence born?

TIBERIO
Sadly, it seems, by the dutchess;
For since he left the court,
For the most part she hath kept her private chamber,
No visitants admitted. In the church.
She hath been seen to pay her pure devotions,
Season'd with tears; and sure her sorrow's true,
Or deeply counterfeited; pomp, and state,
And bravery cast off: and she, that lately
Rivall'd Poppaea in her varied shapes,
Or the Egyptian queen, now, widow-like,
In sable colours, as her husband's dangers
Strangled in her the use of any pleasure,
Mourns for his absence.

STEPHANO
It becomes her virtue,
And does confirm what was reported of her.

TIBERIO
You take it right: but, on the other side.
The darling of his mother, Mariana,
As there were an antipathy between
Her and the dutchess' passions; and as
She'd no dependence on her brother's fortune,
She ne'er appear'd so full of mirth.

STEPHANO
'Tis strange.

[Enter **GRACCHO** with **FIDDLERS**.

But see! her favourite, and accompanied,
To your report.

GRACCHIO
You shall scrape, and I will sing
A scurvy ditty to a scurvy tune,
Repine who dares.

1ST FIDDLER
But if we should offend,
The dutchess having silenced us; and these lords
Stand by to hear us.

GRACCHO
They in name are lords
But I am one in power: and, for the dutchess,
But yesterday we were merry for her pleasure,
We now 'll be for my lady's.

TIBERIO
Signior Graccho.

GRACCHO
A poor man, sir, a servant to the princess;
But you, great lords and counsellors of state,
Whom I stand bound to reverence.

TIBERIO
Come; we know
You are a man in grace.

GRACCHO
Fie! no: I grant,
I bear my fortunes patiently; serve the princess,
And have access at all times to her closet,
Such is my impudence! when your grave lordships
Are masters of the modesty to attend
Three hours, nay sometimes four; and then bid wait
Upon her the next morning.

STEPHANO
He derides us.

TIBERIO
Pray you, what news is stirring? you know all.

GRACCHO
Who, I? alas! I've no intelligence
At home nor abroad; I only sometimes guess
The change of the times: I should ask of your lordships,

Who are to keep their honours, who to lose them;
Who the dutchess smiled on last, or on whom frown'd,
You only can resolve me; we poor waiters
Deal, as you see, in mirth, and foolish fiddles:
It is our element; and could you tell me
What point of state 'tis that I am commanded
To muster up this music, on mine honesty,
You should much befriend me.

STEPHANO
Sirrah, you grow saucy.

TIBERIO
And would be laid by the heels.

GRACCHO
Not by your lordships,
Without a special warrant; look to your own stakes;
Were I committed, here come those would bail me:
Perhaps, we might change places too.

[Enter **ISABELLA**, and **MARIANA**; **GRACCHO** whispers the latter.

TIBERIO
The princess!
We must be patient.

STEPHANO
There is no contending.

TIBERIO
See, the informing rogue!

STEPHANO
That we should stoop
To such a mushroom!

MARIANA
Thou dost mistake; they durst not
Use the least word of scorn, although provoked,
To anything of mine. Go, get you home,
And to your servants, friends, and flatterers, number
How many descents you're noble: look to your wives too;
The smooth-chinned courtiers are abroad.

TIBERIO
No way to be a freeman!

[Exeunt **TIBERIO** and **STEPHANO**.

GRACCHO
Your Excellence hath the best gift to dispatch
These arras pictures of nobility,
I ever read of.

MARIANA
I can speak sometimes.

GRACCHO
And cover so your bitter pills with sweetness
Of princely language to forbid reply,
They are greedily swallow'd.

ISABELLA
But the purpose, daughter,
That brings us hither? Is it to bestow
A visit on this woman, that, because
She only would be thought truly to grieve
The absence and the dangers of my son,
Proclaims a general sadness?

MARIANA
If to vex her
May be interpreted to do her honour,
She shall have many of them. I'll make use
Of my short reign: my lord now governs all;
And she shall know that her idolater,
My brother, being not by now to protect her
I am her equal.

GRACCHO
Of a little thing,
It is so full of gall! A devil of this size,
Should they run for a wager to be spiteful,
Gets not a horse-head of her. [Aside

MARIANA
On her birthday,
We were forced to be merry, and now she's musty,
We must be sad, on pain of her displeasure
We will, we will! this is her private chamber
Where, like an hypocrite, not a true turtle,
She seems to mourn her absent mate; he: servants
Attending her like mutes: but I'll speak to her.
And in a high key too. Play anything
That's light and loud enough but to tormenting her,

And we will have rare sport.

[Music and a song,

[**MARCELIA** appears at a window above, in black.

ISABELLA
She frowns as if
Her looks could fright us.
May it please your greatness, that your late physic hath not work'd;
And that breeds melancholy, as your doctor tells us:
To purge which, we, that are born your highness' vassals,
And are to play the fool to do you service,
Present you with a fit of mirth. What think you
Of a new antic?

ISABELLA
Twould shew rare in ladies.

MARIANA
Being intended for so sweet a creature,
Were she but pleased to grace it.

ISABELLA
Fie! she will,
Be it ne'er so mean; she's made of courtesy.

MARIANA
The mistress of all hearts. One smile, I pray you,
On your poor servants, or a fiddler's fee;
Coming from those fair hands, though but a ducat,
We will enshrine it as a holy relic.

ISABELLA
'Tis wormwood, and it works.

MARCELIA
If I lay by
My fears and griefs, in which you should be sharers,
If doting age could let you but remember,
You have a son; or frontless impudence,
You are a sister; and, in making answer
To what was most unfit for you to speak,
Or me to hear, borrow of my just anger

ISABELLA
A set speech, on my life.
A fart. Penn'd by her chaplain.

MARCELIA

Yes, it can speak, without instruction speak,
And tell your want of manners, that you are rude,
And saucily rude, too.

GRACCHO

Now the game begins.

MARCELIA

You durst not, else, on any hire or hope,
Remembering what I am, and whose I am,
Put on the desperate boldness, to disturb
The least of my retirements.

MARIANA

Note her, now.

MARCELIA

For both shall understand, though the one presume
Upon the privilege due to a mother,
The duke stands now on his own legs, and needs
No nurse to lead him.

ISABELLA

How, a nurse!

MARCELIA

A dry one,
And useless too: but I am merciful,
And dotage signs your pardon.

ISABELLA

I defy thee;
Thee, and thy pardons, proud one!

MARCELIA

For you, puppet

MARIANA

What of me, pine-tree!

MARCELIA

Little you are, I grant,
And have as little worth, but much less wit;
You durst not else, the duke being wholly mine,
His power and honour mine, and the allegiance,
You owe him as a subject, due to me

MARIANA
To you?

MARCELIA
To me: and therefore, as a vassal,
From this hour learn to serve me, or you'll feel
I must make use of my authority,
And, as a princess, punish it.

ISABELLA
A princess!

MARIANA
I had rather be a slave unto a
Moor,
Than know thee for my equal.

ISABELLA
Scornful thing!
Proud of a white face.

MARIANA
Let her but remember
The issue in her leg.

ISABELLA
The charge she puts
The state to, for perfumes.

MARIANA
And howsoe'er
She seems, when she's made up, as she's herself,
She stinks above the ground. O that I could reach you!
The little one you scorn so, with her nails
Would tear your painted face, and scratch those eyes out.
Do but come down.

MARCELIA
Were there no other way,
Just leaping on thy neck, to break my own,
Rather than be outbraved thus.

[She retires.

GRACCHO
Forty ducats
Upon the little hen; she's of the kind,

And will not leave the pit. [Aside.

MARIANA
That it were lawful
To meet her with a poniard and a pistol!
But these weak hands shall shew my spleen

[Re-enter **MARCELIA** below.

MARCELIA
Where are you,
You modicum, you dwarf!

MARIANA
Here, giantess, here.

[Enter **FRANCISCO**, **TIBERIO**, **STEPHANO**, and **GUARDS**.

FRANCISCO
A tumult in the court!

MARIANA
Let her come on.

FRANCISCO
What wind hath raised this tempest?
Sever them, I command you. What's the cause?
Speak, Mariana.

MARIANA
I am out of breath
But we shall meet, we shall? And do you hear, sir!
Or right me on this monster, (she's three feet
Too high for a woman,) or ne'er look to have
A quiet hour with me.

ISABELLA
If my son were here,
And would endure this, may a mother's curse
Pursue and overtake him!

FRANCISCO
O forbear:
On me he's present, both in power and will;
And, madam, I much grieve that, in his absence,
There should arise the least distaste to move you;
It being his principal, nay, only charge,
To have you in his absence, served and honour' d,

As when himself perform 'd the willing office.

MARIANA
This is fine, i' faith.

GRACCHO
I would I were well off!

FRANCISCO
And therefore, I beseech you, madam, frown not,
Till most unwittingly he hath deserved it,
On your poor servant; to your excellence
I ever was and will be such; and lay
The duke's authority, trusted to me,
With willingness at your feet.

MARIANA
O base!

ISABELLA
We are like
To have an equal judge!

FRANCISCO
But, should I find
That you are touch'd in any point of honour,
Or that the least neglect is fall'n upon you,
I then stand up a prince.

1ST FIDDLER
Without reward,
Pray you dismiss us.

GRACCHO
Would I were five leagues hence!

FRANCISCO
I will be partial
To none, not to myself;
Be you but pleased to shew me my offence,
Or if you hold me in your good opinion,
Name those that have offended you.

ISABELLA
I am one,
And I will justify it.

MARIANA

Thou art a base fellow,
To take her part.

FRANCISCO
Remember, she's the dutchess.

MARCELIA
But used with more contempt, than if I were
A peasant's daughter; baited, and hooted at,
Like to a common strumpet; with loud noises
Forced from my prayers; and my private chamber,
Which with all willingness, I would make my prison
During the absence of my lord, denied me:
But if he e'er return.

FRANCISCO
Were you an actor
In this lewd comedy?

MARIANA
Ay, marry was I;
And will be one again.

ISABELLA
I'll join with her,
Though you repine at it.

FRANCISCO
Think not, then, I speak,
For I stand bound to honour, and to serve you;
But that the duke, that lives in this great lady,
For the contempt of him in her, commands you
To be close prisoners.

ISABELLA & MARIANA
Prisoners!

FRANCISCO
Bear them hence;
This is your charge, my lord Tiberio,
And, Stephano, this is yours.

MARCELIA
I am not cruel,
But pleased they may have liberty.

ISABELLA
Pleased, with a mischief!

MARIANA
I'll rather live in any loathsome dungeon,
Than in a paradise at her entreaty:
And, for you, upstart

STEPHANO
There is no contending.

TIBERIO
What shall become of these?

FRANCISCO
See them well whipp'd,
As you will answer it.

TIBERIO
Now, signior Graccho,
What think you of your greatness?

GRACCHO
I preach patience,
And must endure my fortune.

1ST FIDDLER
I was never yet
At such a hunt's-up, nor was so rewarded.

[Exeunt all but **FRANCISCO** and **MARCELIA**.

FRANCISCO
Let them first know themselves, and how you are
To be served and honour'd; which, when they confess,
You may again receive them to your favour:
And then it will shew nobly.

MARCELIA
With my thanks
The duke shall pay you his, if he return
To bless us with his presence.

FRANCISCO
There is nothing
That can be added to your fair acceptance;
That is the prize, indeed; all else are blanks,
And of no value. As, in virtuous actions,
The undertaker finds a full reward,
Although conferr'd upon unthankful men;

So, any service done to so much sweetness,
However dangerous, and subject to
An ill construction in your favour finds
A wish'd, and glorious end.

MARCELIA
From you, I take this
As loyal duty; but, in any other,
It would appear gross flattery.

FRANCISCO
Flattery, madam!
You are so rare and excellent in all things,
And raised so high upon a rock of goodness,
As that vice cannot reach you; who but looks on
This temple, built by nature to perfection,
But must bow to it; and out of that zeal,
Not only learn to adore it, but to love it?

MARCELIA [Aside]
Whither will this fellow?

FRANCISCO
Pardon, therefore, madam,
If an excess in me of humble duty,
Teach me to hope, and though it be not in
The power of man to merit such a blessing,
My piety, for it is more than love,
May find reward.

MARCELIA
You have it in my thanks;
And, on my hand, I am pleased that you shall take
A full possession of it: but, take heed
That you fix here, and feed no hope beyond it;
If you do, it will prove fatal.

FRANCISCO
Be it death,
And death with torments tyrants ne'er found out,
Yet I must say, I love you.

MARCELIA
As a subject;
And 'twill become you.

FRANCISCO
Farewell, circumstance!

And since you are not pleased to understand me,
But by a plain and usual form of speech;
All superstitious reverence laid by,
I love you as a man, and, as a man,
I would enjoy you. Why do you start, a fly me?
I am no monster, and you but a woman,
A woman made to yield, and by example
Told it is lawful: favours of this nature
Are, in our age, no miracles in the greates
And, therefore, lady

MARCELIA
Keep off! O you Powers!—
Libidinous beast! and, add to that, u thankful!
A crime, which creatures wanting reason, fly from.
Are all the princely bounties, favours honours,
Which, with some prejudice to his own wisdom,
Thy lord and raiser hath conferr'd upon thee,
In three days' absence buried? Hath I made thee,
A thing obscure, almost without a name,
The envy of great fortunes? Have I graced thee,
Beyond thy rank, and entertain'd thee, as
A friend, and not a servant? And is this,
This impudent attempt ,to taint mine honour,
The fair return of both our ventured favour!

FRANCISCO
Hear my excuse.

MARCELIA
The devil may plead mercy,
And, with as much assurance, as thou yield one!
Burns lust so hot in thee? or is thy pride
Grown up to such a height, that, but princess,
No woman can content thee; and, add to it
His wife and princess, to whom thou art tied
In all the bonds of duty—Read my life,
And find one act of mine so loosely carried,
That could invite a most self-loving fool,
Set off with all that fortune could throw on him,
To the least hope to find way to my favour;
And what's the worst mine enemies could wish me,
I'll be thy strumpet.

FRANCISCO
'Tis acknowledged, madam,
That your whole course of life hath been a pattern
For chaste and virtuous women. In your beauty,

Which I first saw, and loved, as a fair crystal,
I read' your heavenly mind, clear and untainted;
And while the duke did prize you to your value,
Could it have been in man to pay that duty,
I well might envy him, but durst not hope
To stop you in your full career of goodness:
But now I find that he's fall'n from his fortune,
And, howsoever he would appear doting,
Grown cold in his affection; I presume,
From his most barbarous neglect of you,
To offer my true service. Nor stand I bound,
To look back on the courtesies of him,
That, of all living men, is most unthankful.

MARCELIA
Unheard-of impudence!

FRANCISCO
You'll say I am modest,
When I have told the story. Can he tax me,
That have received some worldly trifles from him,
For being ungrateful; when he, that first tasted,
And hath so long enjoy'd, your sweet embraces,
In which all blessings that our frail condition
Is capable of, are wholly comprehended,
As cloy'd with happiness, contemns the giver
Of his felicity; and, as he reach 'd not
The masterpiece of mischief which he aims at,
Unless he pay those favours he stands bound to,
With fell and deadly hate! You think he loves 'you
With unexampled fervour; nay, dotes on you,
As there were something in you more than woman:
When, on my knowledge, he long since hath wish'd
You were among the dead; and I, you scorn so,
Perhaps, am your preserver.

MARCELIA
Bless me, good angels,
Or I am blasted! Lies so false and wicked,
And fashion'd to so damnable a purpose,
Cannot be spoken by a human tongue.
My husband hate me! give thyself the lie,
False and accurs'd! Thy soul, if thou hast any,
Can witness, never lady stood so bonnd
To the unfeign'd affection of her lord,
As I do to my Sforza. If thou wouldst work
Upon my weak credulity, tell me, rather,
That the earth moves; the sun and stars stand still;

The ocean keeps nor floods nor ebbs; or that
There's peace between the lion and the lamb;
Or that the ravenous eagle and the dove
Keep in one aerie, and bring up their young;
Or anything that is averse to nature:
And I will sooner credit it, than that
My lord can think of me, but as a jewel,
He loves more than himself, and all the world.

FRANCISCO
O innocence abused! simplicity cozen'd!
It were a sin, for which we have no name,
To keep you longer in this wilful error.
Read his affection here;—

[Gives her a paper.

—and then observe
How dear he holds you! 'Tis his character,
Which cunning yet could never counterfeit.

MARCELIA
'Tis his hand, I'm resolv'd of it.
I'll try
What the inscription is.

FRANCISCO
Pray you, do so.
Marc, [reads]
You know my pleasure, and the hour of Marcelia s death, which fait not to execute, as you will answer
the contrary, not with your head alone, but with the ruin of your whole family. And this, written with
mine own hand, and signed with my privy signet, shall be your sufficient warrant.
LODOVICO SFORZA.
I do obey it! every word's a poniard,
And reaches to my heart.

[Swoons.

FRANCISCO
What have I done?
Madam! for heaven's sake, madam! O my fate!
I'll bend her body: this is yet some pleasure:
I'll kiss her into a new life. Dear lady!
She stirs. For the duke's sake, for Sforza's sake

MARCELIA
Sforza's! stand off; though dead,
I will be his,

And even my ashes shall abhor the touch
Of any other. O unkind, and cruel!
Learn, women, learn to trust in one another r
There is no faith in man: Sforza is false,
False to Marcelia!

FRANCISCO
But I am true,
And live to make you happy, i All the pomp.
State, and observance you had, being his,
Compared to what you shall enjoy, when mine,
Shall be no more remember 'd. Lose his memory,
And look with cheerful beams on your new creature;
And know, what he hath plotted for your good,
Fate cannot alter. If the emperor
Take not his life, at his return he dies.
And by my hand: my wife, that is his heir,
Shall quickly follow: then we reign alone!
For with this arm I'll swim through seas of blood,
Or make a bridge, arch'd with the bones of men,
But I will grasp my aims in you, my dearest,
Dearest, and best of women!

MARCELIA
Thou art a villain!
All attributes of arch- villains made into one,
Cannot express thee, I prefer the hate
Of Storza, though it mark me for the grave,
Before thy base affection. I am yet
Pure and unspotted in my true love to him;
Nor shall it be corrupted, though he's tainted:
Nor will I part with innocence, because
He is found guilty. For thyself, thou art
A tiling, that, equal with the devil himself,
I do detest and scorn.

FRANCISCO
Thou, then, art nothing:
Thy life is in my power, disdainful woman!
Think on't, and tremble.

MARCELIA
No, though thou wert now
To play thy hangman's part. Thou well may'st be
My executioner, and art only fit
For such employment; but ne'er hope to have
The least grace from me. I will never see thee,
Just as the shame of men: so, with my curses

Of horror to thy conscience in this life,
And pains in hell hereafter, I spit at thee;
And, making haste to make my peace with heaven,
Expect thee as my hangman.

[Exit.

FRANCISCO
I am lost
In the discovery of this fatal secret.
Cursd hope, that flatter'd me, that wrongs could make her
A stranger to her goodness! all my plots
Turn back upon myself; but I am in,
And must go on: and, since I have put off
From the shore of innocence, guilt be now my pilot!
Revenge first wrought me; murder's his twin brother:
One deadly sin, then, help to cure another!

[Exit.

ACT III

SCENE I. The Imperial Camp, Before Pavia

Enter **MEDINA**, **HERNANDO**, and **ALPHONSO**.

MEDINA
The spoil, the spoil! 'tis that the soldier fights for.
Our victory, as yet, affords us nothing
But wounds and empty honour. We have poss'd
The hazard of a dreadful day, and forced
A passage with our swords through all the dangers
That, page-like, wait on the success of war;
And now expect reward.

HERNANDO
Hell put in
The enemy's mind to be desperate, and hold out!
Yieldings and compositions will undo us;
And what is that way given, for the most part,
Comes to the emperor's coffers to defray,
The charge of the great action, as 'tis rumour'd
When, usually, some thing in grace, that ne'er heard
The cannon's roaring tongue, but at a triumph,
Puts in, and for his intercession shares,
All that we fought for; the poor soldier left

To starve, or fill up hospitals.

ALPHONSO
But, when
We enter towns by force, and carve ourselves,
Pleasure with pillage and the richest wines
Open our shrunk-up veins, and pour into them
New blood and fervour

MEDINA
I long to be at it;
To see these chuffs, that every day may spend
A soldier's entertainment for a year,
Yet make a third meal of a bunch of raisins;
These sponges, that suck up a kingdom's fat,
Battening like scarabs in the dung of peace,
To be squeezed out by the rough hand of war;
And all that their whole lives have heap'd together,
By cozenage, perjury, or sordid thrift,
With one gripe to be ravish'd.

HERNANDO
I would be tousing
Their fair madonas, that in little dogs,
Monkeys, and paraquittos, consume thousands;
Yet, for the advancement of a noble action,
Repine to part with a poor piece of eight:
War's plagues upon them! I have seen them stop
Their scornful noses first, then seem to swoon,
At sight of a buff jerkin, if it were not
Perfumed, and hid with gold: yet these nice wantons,
Spurr'd on by lust, cover'd in some disguise
To meet some rough court-stallion, and be leap'd,
Durst enter into any common brothel,
Though all varieties of stink contend there;
Yet praise the entertainment.

MEDINA
I may live
To see the tatter 'd'st rascals of my troop
Drag them out of their closets, with a vengeance!
When neither threat 'ning, flattering, kneeling, howling,
Can ransome one poor jewel, or redeem
Themselves, from their blunt wooing.

HERNANDO
My main hope is,
To begin the sport at Milan: there's enough,

And of all kinds of pleasure we can wish for,
To satisfy the most covetous.

ALPHONSO
Every day
We look for a remove.

MEDINA
For Lodowick Sforza,
The duke of Milan, I, on mine own knowledge,
Can say thus much: he is too much a soldier,
Too confident of his own worth, too rich too,
And understands too well the emperor hates him,
To hope for composition.

ALPHONSO
On my life,
We need not fear his coming in.

HERNANDO
On mine,
I do not wish it: I had rather that,
To shew his valou'r, he'd put us to the trouble
To fetch him in by the ears.

MEDINA
The emperor!

[Flourish. Enter **CHARLES**, **PESCARA**, and **ATTENDANTS**.

CHARLES
You make me wonder: nay, it is no counsel,
You may partake it, gentlemen: who'd have thought,
That he, that scorn'd our proffer'd amity
When he was sued to, should, ere he be summon'd,
(Whether persuaded to it by base fear,
Or flatter'd by false hope, which, 'tis uncertain,)
First kneel for mercy?

MEDINA
When your majesty
Shall please to instruct us who it is, we may
Admire it with you.

CHARLES
Who, but the duke of Milan,
The right hand of the French! of all that stand
In our displeasure, whom necessity

Compels to seek our favour, I would have sworn
Sforza had been the last.

HERNANDO
And should be writ so,
In the list of those you pardon. Would his city
Had rather held us out a siege, like Troy,
Than, by a feign'd submission, he should cheat you
Of a just revenge; or us, of those fair glories
We have sweat blood to purchase!

MEDINA
With your honour
You cannot hear him.

ALPHONSO
The sack alone of Milan
Will pay the army.

CHARLES
I am not so weak,
To be wrought on, as you fear! nor ignorant
That money is the sinew of the war;
And on what terms soever he seek peace,
'Tis in our power to grant it, or deny it:
Yet, for our glory, and to shew him that
We've brought him on his knees, it is resolved
To hear him as a suppliant. Bring him in;
But let him see the effects of our just anger,
In the guard that you make for him.

[Exit **PESCARA**.

HERNANDO
I am now
Familiar with the issue; all plagues on it!
He will appear in some dejected habit,
His countenance suitable, and, for his order,
A rope about his neck: then kneel and tell
Old stories, what a worthy thing it is
To have the power, and not to use it; then add to that
A tale of king Tigranes, and great Pompey,
Who said, forsooth, and wisely! 'twas more honour
To make a king than killone; which, applied
To the emperor, and himself, a pardon's granted
To him an enemy; and we, his servants,
Condemn'd to 'beggary. [Aside to **MEDINA**.

MEDINA
Yonder he comes;
But not as you expected.

[Re-enter **PESCARA** with **SFORZA**, strongly guarded.

ALPHONSO
He looks as if
He would outface his dangers.

HERNANDO
I am cozen 'd:
A suitor, in the devil's name!

MEDINA
Hear him speak.

SFORZA
I come not, emperor, to invade thy mercy,
By fawning on thy fortune; nor bring with me
Excuses, or denials. I profess,
And with a good man's confidence, even this instant
That I am in thy power, I was thine enemy;
Thy deadly and vow'd enemy: one that wish'd
Confusion to thy person and estates;
And witli my utmost powers, and deepest counsels,
Had they been truly follow'd, further'd it.
Nor will I now, although my neck were under
The hangman's axe, with one poor syllable
Confess, but that I honour 'd the French king,
More than thyself, and all men.

MEDINA
By Saint Jacques,
This is no flattery.

HERNANDO
There is fire and spirit in't;
But not long-lived, I hope,

SFORZA
Now give me leave,
My hate against thyself, and love to him
Freely acknowledged, to give up the reasons
That make me so affected: In my wants
I ever found him faithful; had supplies
Of men and monies from him; and my hopes,
Quite sunk, were, by his grace, buoy'd up again;

He was, indeed, to me, as my good angel
To guard me from all dangers. I dare speak,
Nav, must and will, his praise now, in as high
And loud a key, as when he was thy equal.
The benefits he sow'd in me, met not
Unthankful ground, but yielded him his own
With fair increase, and I still glory in it.
And, though my fortunes, poor, compared to his,
And Milan, weigh'd with France, appear as nothing,
Are in thy fury burnt, let it be mention'd,
They served but as small tapers to attend
The solemn flame at this great funeral;
And with them I will gladly waste myself,
Rather than undergo the imputation
Of being base, or unthankful.

ALPHONSO
Nobly spoken!

HERNANDO
I do begin, I know not why, to hate him
Less than I did.

SFORZA
If that, then, to be grateful
For courtesies received, or not to leave
A friend in his necessities, be a crime
Amongst you Spaniards, which other nations
That, like you, aim'd at empire, loved, and cherish d
Where'er they found it, Sforza brings his head
To pay the forfeit. Nor come I as a slave,
Pinion'd and fetter'd, in a squalid weed,
Falling before thy feet, kneeling and howling,
For a forestall'd remission: that were poor,
And would but shame thy victory; for conquest
Over base foes, is a captivity,
And not a triumph. I ne'er feared to die,
More than I wish'd to live. When I had reach'd
My ends in being a duke, I wore these robes,
This crown upon my head, and to my side
This sword was girt; and witness truth, that, now
'Tis in another's power, when I shall part
With them and life together, I'm the same:
My veins then did not swell with pride; nor now
Shrink they for fear. Know, sir, that Sforza stands
Prepared for either fortune.

HERNANDO

As I live,
I do begin strangely to love this fellow;
And could part with three quarters of my share in
The promised spoil, to save him.

SFORZA
But, if example
Of my fidelity to the French, whose honours,
Titles, and glories, are now mix'd with yours,
As brooks, devour'd by rivers, lose their names,
Has power to invite you to make him a friend,
That hath given evident proof he knows to love,
And to be thankful: this my crown, now yours,
You may restore me, and in me instruct
These brave commanders, should your fortune change,
Which now I wish not, what they may expect
From noble enemies, for being faithful.
The charges of the war I will defray,
And, what you may, not without hazard, force,
Bring freely to you: I'll prevent the cries
Of murder'd infants, and of ravish'd maids,
Which in a city sack'd, call on heaven's justice,
And stop the course of glorious victories:
And, when I know the captains and the soldiers,
That have in the late battle done best service,
And are to be rewarded, I myself,
According to their quality and merits,
Will see them largely recompensed. I have said,
And now expect my sentence.

ALPHONSO
By this light,
Tis a brave gentleman.

MEDINA
How like a block
The emperor sits!

HERNANDO
He hath deliver'd reasons,
Especially in his purpose to enrich
Such as fought bravely, (I myself am one,
I care not who knows it,) as I wonder that
He can be so stupid. Now he begins to stir:
Mercy, an't be thy will!

CHARLES
Thou hast so far

Outgone my expectation, noble Sforza,
For such I hold thee; and true constancy,
Raised on a brave foundation, bears such palm
And privilege with it, that where we behold it,
Though in an enemy, it does command us
To love and honour it. By my future hopes,
I am glad for thy sake, that in seeking favour,
Thou did'st not borrow of vice her indirect,
Crooked, and abject means, and for mine own,
That, since my purposes must now be changed
Touching thy life and fortunes, the world cannot
Tax me of levity in my settled counsels;
I being neither wrought by tempting bribes,
Nor servile flattery; but forced into it
By a fair war of virtue.

HERNANDO
This sounds well.

CHARLES
All former passages of hate be buried:
For thus with open arms I meet thy love,
And as a friend embrace it; 'and so far
I am from robbing thee of the least honour,
That with my hands, to make it sit the faster,
I set thy crown once more upon thy head;
And do not only style thee, Duke of Milan,
But vow to keep thee so. Yet, not to take
From others to give only to myself,
I will not hinder your magnificence
To my commanders, neither will I urge it;
But in that, as in all things else, I leave you
To be your own disposer.

[Flourish. Exit with **ATTENDANTS**.

SFORZA
May I live
To seal my loyalty, though with loss of life,
In some brave service worthy Caesar's favour,
I shall die most happy! Gentlemen,
Receive me to your loves; and, if henceforth
There can arise a difference between us,
It shall be in a noble emulation
Who hath the fairest sword, or dare go farthest,
To fight for Charles the emperor.

HERNANDO

We embrace you,
As one well read in all the points of honour:
And there we are your scholars.

SFORZA
True; but such
As far outstrip the master. We'll contend
Ln love hereafter: in the meantime, pray you,
Let me discharge my debt, and, as an earnest
Of what's to come, divide this cabinet:
In the small body of it there are jewels
Will yield a hundred thousand pistolets,
Which honour me to receive.

MEDINA
You bind us to you.

SFORZA
And when great Charles commands me to his presence,
If you will please to excuse my abrupt departure,
Designs that most concern me, next this mercy,
Calling me home, I shall hereafter meet you,
And gratify the favour.

HERNANDO
In this, and all things,
We are your servants.

SFORZA
A name I ever owe you.

[Exeunt **MEDINA**, **HERNANDO**, and **ALPHONSO**.

PESCARA
So, sir; this tempest is well overblown,
And all things fall out to our wishes: but,
In my opinion, this quick return,
Before you've made a party in the court
Among the great ones, (for these needy captains
Have little power in peace,) may beget danger,
At least suspicion.

SFORZA
Where true honour lives,
Doubt hath no being: I desire no pawn
Beyond an emperor's word, for my assurance.
Besides, Pescara, to thyself, of all men,
I will confess my weakness: though my state

And crown's restored me, though I am in grace,
And that a little stay might be a step
To greater honours, I must hence. Alas!
I live not here; my wife, my wife, Pescara,
Being absent, I am dead. Prithee, excuse,
And do not chide, for friendship's sake, my fondness,
But ride along with me; I'll give you reasons,
And strong ones, to plead for me.

PESCARA
Use your own pleasure;
I'll bear you company,

SFORZA
Farewell, grief! I am stored with
Two blessings most desired in human life,
A constant friend, an unsuspected wife.

[Exeunt.

SCENE II. Milan. A Room in the Castle.

Enter an **OFFICER** with **GRACCHO**.

OFFICER
What I did, I had warrant for; you have tasted
My office gently, and for those soft strokes,
Flea-bitings to the jerks I could have lent you,
There does belong a feeing.

GRACCHO
Must I pay
For being tormented, and dishonour'd?

OFFICER
Fie! no,
Your honour's not impair'd in't. What's the letting out
Of a little corrupt blood, and the next way too?
There is no surgeon like me, to take off
A courtier's itch that's rampant at great ladies,
Or turns knave for preferment, or grows proud
Of his rich cloaks and suits, though got by brokage,
And so forgets his betters.

GRACCHO
Very good, sir:

But am I the first man of quality
That e'er came under your fingers?

OFFICER
Not by a thousand;
And they have' said I have a lucky hand too:
Both men and women of all sorts have bow'd
Under this sceptre. I have had a fellow
That could endite, forsooth, and make fine metres
To tinkle in the ears of ignorant madams,
That, for defaming of great men, was sent me
Threadbare and lousy, and in three days after,
Discharged by another that set him on. I have seen him
Cap a pie gallant, and his stripes wash'd off
With oil of angels.

GRACCHO
'Twas a sovereign cure.

OFFICER
There was a sectary too, that would not be
Conformable to the orders of the church,
Nor yield to any argument of reason,
But still rail at authority, brought to me,
When I had worm'd his tongue, and truss'd his haunches,
Grew a fine pulpit man, and was beneficed:
Had he not cause to thank me?

GRACCHO
There was physic
Was to the purpose.

OFFICER
Now, for women, sir,
For your more consolation, I could tell you
Twenty fine stories, but I'll end in one,
And 'tis the last that's memorable.

GRACCHO
Prithee, do;
For I grow weary of thee.

OFFICER
There was lately
A fine she-waiter in the court, that doted
Extremely of a gentleman, that had
His main dependence on a signior's favour
I will not name, but could not corn-pass him

On any terms. This wanton, at dead midnight,
Was found at the exercise behind the arras,
With the 'foresaid signior: he got clear off,
But she was seized on, and, to save his honour,
Endured the lash; and, though I made her often
Curvet and caper, she would never tell
Who play'd at pushpin with her.

GRACCHO
But what follow'd?
Prithee be brief.

OFFICER
Why this, sir: She delivered,
Had store of crowns assign'd her by her patron,
Who forced the gentleman, to save her credit,
To marry her, and say he was the party
Found in Lob's pound: so she, that, before, gladly
Would have been his whore, reigns o'er him as his wife;
Nor dares he grumble at it. Speak but truth, then,
Is not my office lucky?

GRACCHO
Go, there's for thee;
But what will be my fortune?

OFFICER
If you thrive not
After that soft correction, come again.

GRACCHO
I thank you, knave.

OFFICER
And then, knave, I will fit you.

GRACCHO
Whipt like a rogue! no lighter punishment serve
To balance with a little mirth! 'Tis well;
My credit sunk for ever, I am now
Fit company only for pages and for footboys.
That have perused the porter's lodge.

[Enter **JULIO** and **GIOVANNI**.

GIOVANNI
See, Julio,
Yonder the proud slave is. How he looks now,

After his castigation!

JULIO
As he came
From a close fight at sea under the hatches,
With a she-Dunkirk, that was shot before
Between wind and water; and he hath sprung a leak too,
Or I am cozen'd.

GIOVANNI
Let's be merry with him.

GRACCHO
How they stare at me! am I turn'd to an owl?
The wonder, gentlemen?

JULIO
I read, this morning,
Strange stories of the passive fortitude
Of men in former ages, which I thought
Impossible, and not to be believed:
But now I look on you, my wonder ceases.

GRACCHO
The reason, sir?

JULIO
Why, sir, you have been whipt,
Whipt, signior Graccho; and the whip, I take it,
Is to a gentleman, the greatest trial
That may be of his patience.

GRACCHO
Sir, I'll call you
To a strict account for this.

GIOVANNI
I'll not deal with you,
Unless I have a beadle for my second;
And then I'll answer you.

JULIO
Farewell, poor Graccho.

[Exeunt **JULIO** and **GIOVANNI**.

GRACCHO
Better and better still. If ever wrongs

Could teach a wretch to find the way to vengeance,

[Enter **FRANCISCO** and a **SERVANT**.

Hell now inspire me! How, the lord protector!
My judge; I thank him! Whither thus in private?
I will not see him.

[Stands aside.

FRANCISCO
If I am sought for,
Say I am indisposed, and will not hear
Or suits, or suitors.

SERVANT
But, sir, if the princess
Enquire, what shall I answer?

FRANCISCO
Say, I am rid
Abroad to take the air; but by no means
Let her know I'm in court.

SERVANT
So I shall tell her.

[Exit.

FRANCISCO
Within there, ladies!

[Enter a **GENTLE-WOMAN**.

GENTLE-WOMAN
My good lord, your pleasure?

FRANCISCO
Prithee, let me beg thy favour for access
To the dutchess.

GENTLE-WOMAN
In good sooth, my lord, I dare not;
She's very private.

FRANCISCO
Come, there's gold to buy thee
A new gown, and a rich one.

GENTLE-WOMAN
I once swore
If e'er I lost my maidenhead, it should be
With a great lord, as you are; and, I know not how,
I feel a yielding inclination in me,
If you have appetite.

FRANCISCO
Pox on, thy maidenhead!
Wiere is thy lady?

GENTLE-WOMAN
If you venture on her,
She's walking in the gallery; perhaps,
You will find her less tractable.

FRANCISCO
Bring me to her.

GENTLE-WOMAN
I fear, you'll have cold entertainment, when
You are at your journey's end; and 'twere discretion
To take a snatch by the way.

FRANCISCO
Prithee, leave fooling:
My page waits in the lobby; give him sweetmeats;
He is train'd up for his master's ease,
And he will cool thee.

[Exeunt **FRANCISCO**, and **GENTLE-WOMAN**.

GRACCHO
A brave discovery beyond my hope,
A plot even ofter'd to my hand to work on!
If I am dull now, may I live and die
The scorn of worms and slaves! Let me consider:
My lady and her mother first committed,
In the favour of the dutchess; and I whipt!
That, with an iron pen, is writ in brass
On my tough heart, now grown a harder metal.
And all his bribed approaches to the dutchess
To be conceal'd! good, good. This to my lady
Deliver'd, as I'll order it, runs her mad.
But this may prove but courtship! let it be,
I care not, so it feed her jealousy.

[Exit.

Enter **MARCELIA** and **FRANCISCO**.

MARCELIA
Believe thy tears or oaths! can it be hoped,
After a practice so abhorr'd and horrid,
Repentance e'er can find thee?

FRANCISCO
Dearest lady,
Great in your fortune, greater in your goodness,
Make a superlative of excellence,
In being greatest in your saving mercy.
I do confess, humbly confess my fault,
To be beyond all pity; my attempt
So barbarously rude, that it would turn
A saint-like patience into savage fury.
But you, that are all innocence and virtue.
No spleen or anger in you of a woman,
But when a holy zeal to piety fires you,
May, if you please, impute the fault to Jove!
Or call it beastly lust, for 'tis no better.
A sin, a monstrous sin! yet with it many
That did prove good men after, have been tempted;
And, though I'm crooked now, 'tis in your power
To make me straight again.

MARCELIA
Is't possible
This can be cunning! [Aside.

FRANCISCO
But, if no submission,
Nor prayers can appease you, that you may know
Tis not the fear of death that makes me sue thus,
But a loath'd detestation of my madness,
Which makes me wish to live to have your pardon;
I will not wait the sentence of the duke,
Since his return is doubtful, but I myself
Will do a fearful justice on myself,
No witness by but you, there being no more
When I offended. Yet, before I do it,
For I perceive in you no signs of mercy,

I will disclose a secret, which dying with me,
May prove your ruin.

MARCELIA
Speak it; it will take from
The burthen of thy conscience.

FRANCISCO
Thus, then, madam;
The warrant by my lord sign'd for your death,
Was but conditional; but you must swear
By your unspotted truth, not to reveal it,
Or I end here abruptly.

MARCELIA
By my hopes
Of joys hereafter. On.

FRANCISCO
Nor was it hate
That forced him to it, but excess of love.
And, if I ne'er return, (so said great Sforza,)
No living man deserving to enjoy
My best 'Marcelia, with the first neivs
That I am dead, (for no man after me
Must e'er enjoy her,) fail not to kill her
But till certain proof
Assure thee I am lost, (these were his words,)
Observe and honour her, as if the soul
Of -woman s goodness only dwelt in hers.
This trust I have abused, and basely wrong'd;
And, if the excelling pity of your mind
Cannot forgive it, as I dare not hope it,
Rather than look on my offended lord,
I stand resolved to punish it.

[Draws his sword.

MARCELIA
Hold! 'tis forgiven,
And by me freely pardon'd. In thy fair life
Hereafter, study to deserve this bounty,
Which thy true penitence, such I believe it,
Against my resolution hath forced from me.
But that my lord, my Sforza, should esteem
My life fit only as a page, to wait on
The various course of his uncertain fortunes;
Or cherish in himself that sensual hope,

In death to know me as a wife, afflicts me;
For does his envy less deserve mine anger,
Which though, such is my love, I would not nourish,
Will slack the ardour that I had to see him
Return in safety.

FRANCISCO
But if your entertainment
Should give the least ground to his jealousy,
To raise up an opinion I am false,
You then destroy your mercy. Therefore, madam,
(Though I shall ever look on you as on
My life's preserver, and the miracle
Of human pity,) would you but vouchsafe,
In company, to do me those fair graces,
And favours, which your innocence and honour
May safely warrant, it would to the duke,
I being to your best self alone known guilty,
Make me appear most innocent.

MARCELIA
Have your wishes;
And something I may do to try his temper,
At least, to make him know a constant wife
Is not so slaved to her husband's doting humours,
But that she may deserve to live a widow,
Her fate appointing it.

FRANCISCO
It is enough;
Nay, all I could desire, and will make way
To my revenge, which shall disperse itself
On him, on her, and all.

[Aside and exit. Shout and flourish.

MARCELIA
What shout is that?

[Enter **TIBERIO** and **STEPHANO**.

TIBERIO
All happiness to the dutchess, that may flow
From the duke's new and wish'd return!

MARCELIA
He's welcome.

STEPHANO
How coldly she receives it!

TIBERIO
Observe the encounter.

[Flourish. Enter **SFORZA**, **PESCARA**, **ISABELLA**, **MARIANA**, **GRACCHO**, and **ATTENDANTS**.

MARIANA
What you have told me, Graccho, is believed,
And I'll find time to stir in't.

GRACCHO
As you see cause;
I will not do ill offices.

SFORZA
I have stood
Silent thus long, Marcelia, expecting
When, with more than a greedy haste, thou wouldst
Have flown into my arms, and on my lips
Have printed a deep welcome. My desires
To glass myself in these fair eyes, have borne me
With more than human speed: nor durst I stay
In any temple, or to any saint
To pay my vows and thanks for my return,
Till I had' seen thee.

MARCELIA
Sir, I am most happy
To look upon you safe, and would express
My love and duty in a modest fashion,
Such as might suit with the behaviour
Of one that knows herself a wife, and how
To temper her desires, not like a wanton
Fired with hot appetite; nor can it wrong me
To love discreetly.

SFORZA
How! why, can there be
A mean in your affections to Sforza?
Or any act, though ne'er so loose, that may
Invite or heighten appetite, appear
Immodest or uncomely? Do not move me;
My passions to you are in extremes,
And know no bounds: come; kiss me.

MARCELIA

I obey you.

SFORZA
By all the joys of love, she does salute me
As if I were her grandfather! What witch,
With cursed spells, hath quench'd the amorous heat
That lived upon these lips? Tell me, Marcelia,
And truly tell me, is't a fault of mine
That hath begot this coldness? or neglect
Of others, in my absence?

MARCELIA
Neither, sir:
I stand indebted to your substitute,
Noble and good Francisco, for his care
And fair observance of me: there was nothing
With which you, being present, could supply
That I dare say I wanted.

SFORZA
How!

MARCELIA
The pleasures
That sacred Hymen warrants us, excepted,
Of which, in troth, you are too great a doter;
And there is more of beast in it than man.
Let us love temperately; things violent last not,
And too much dotage rather argues folly
Than true affection.

GRACCHO
Observe but this,
And how she praised my lord's care and observance;
And then judge, madam, if my intelligence
Have any ground of truth.

MARIANA
No more; I mark it.

STEPHANO
How the duke stands!

TIBERIO
As he were rooted there,
And had no motion.

PESCARA

My lord, from whence
Grows this amazement?

SFORZA
It is more, dear my friend;
For I am doubtful whether I've a being,
But certain that my life's a burden to me.
Take me back, good Pescara, shew me to Caesar
In all his rage and fury; I disclaim
His mercy: to live now, which is his gift,
Is worse than death, and with all studied torments.
Marcelia is unkind, nay, worse, grown cold
In her affection; my excess of fervour,
Which yet was never equall'd, grown distasteful.
But have thy wishes, woman; thou shalt know
That I can be myself, and thus shake off
The fetters of fond dotage. From my sight,
Without reply; for I am apt to do
Something I may repent.

[Exit **MARCELIA**

Oh! who would place
His happiness in most accursed woman,
In whom obsequiousness engenders pride;
And harshness deadly hatred! From this hour
I'll labour to forget there are such creatures;
True friends be now my mistresses. Clear your brows,
And, though my heart-strings crack for't I will be
To all a free example of delight.
We will have sports of all kinds, and propound
Rewards to such as can produce us new;
Unsatisfied, though we surfeit in their store;
And never think of curs'd Marcelia more.

[Exeunt.

ACT IV

SCENE I. The Same. A Room in The Castle

Enter **FRANCISCO** and **GRACCHO**.

FRANCISCO
And is it possible thou shouldst forget

A wrong of such a nature, and then study
My safety and content?

GRACCHO
Sir, but allow me
Only to have read the elements of courtship,
Not the abstruse and hidden arts to thrive there;
And you may please to grant me so much knowledge,
That injuries from one in grace, like you,
Are noble favours. Is it not grown common,
In every sect, for those that want, to suffer
From such as have to give? Your captain cast,
If poor, though not thought daring, but approved so,
To raise a coward into name, that's rich,
Suffers disgraces publicly; but receives
Rewards for them in private.

FRANCISCO
Well observed.
Put on; we'll be familiar, and discourse
A little of this argument. That day,
In which it was first rumour'd, then confirm'd,
Great Sforza thought me worthy of his favour,
I found myself to be another thing;
Not what I was before. I passed then
For a pretty fellow, and of pretty parts too,
And was perhaps received so; but, once raised,
The liberal courtiers made me master of
Those virtues which I ne'er knew in myself:
If I pretended to a jest, 'twas made one
By their interpretation; if I offer'd
To reason of philosophy, though absurdly,
They had helps to save me, and without a blush
Would swear that I, by nature, had more knowledge,
Than others could acquire by any labour:
Nay, all I did, indeed, which in another
Was not remarkable, in me shew'd rarely.

GRACCHO
But then they tasted of your bounty.

FRANCISCO
True:
They gave me those good parts I was not born to,
And, by my intercession, they got that
Which, had I cross'd them, they durst not have hoped for.

GRACCHO

All this is oracle: and shall I, then,
For a foolish whipping, leave to honour him,
That holds the wheel of fortune? no; that savours
Too much of the ancient freedom. Since great men
Receive disgraces and give thanks, poor knaves
Must have nor spleen, nor anger. Though I love
My limbs as well as any man, if you had now
A humour to kick me lame into an office,
Where I might sit in state and undo others,
Stood I not bound to kiss the foot that did it?
Though it seem strange, there have been such things seen
In the memory of man.

FRANCISCO
But to the purpose,
And then, that service done, make thine own fortunes.
My wife, thou say'st, is jealous I am too
Familiar with the dutchess.

GRACCHO
And incensed
For her commitment in her brother's absence;
And by her mother's anger is spurr'd on
To make discovery of it. This her purpose
Was trusted to my charge, which I declined
As much as in me lay; but, finding her
Determinately bent to undertake it,
Though breaking my faith to her may destroy
My credit with your lordship, I yet thought,
Though at my peril, I stood bound to reveal it.

FRANCISCO
I thank thy care, and will deserve this secret,
In making thee acquainted with a greater,
And of more moment. Come into my bosom,
And take it from me: Canst thou think, dull Graccho,
My power and honours were ccnferr'd upon me,
And, add to them, this form, to have my pleasures
Confined and limited? I delight in change,
And sweet variety; that's my heaven on earth,
For which I love life only. I confess,
My wife pleased me a day, the dutchess, two,
(And yet I must not say I have enjoy'd her,)
But now I care for neither: therefore,
Graccho,
So far I am from stopping Mariana
In making her complaint, that I desire thee
To urge her to it.

GRACCHO
That may prove your ruin;
The duke already being, as 'tis reported,
Doubtful she hath play'd false.

FRANCISCO
There thou art cozen'd;
His dotage, like an ague, keeps his course,
And now 'tis strongly on him. But I lose time,
And therefore know, whether thou wilt or no,
Thou art to be my instrument; and, in spite
Of the old saw, that says, It is not safe
On any terms to trust a man that's wrong'd,
I dare thee to be false.

GRACCHO
This is a language,
My lord, I understand- not.

FRANCISCO
You thought, sirrah,
To put a trick on me for the relation
Of what I knew before, and, having won
Some weighty secret from me, in revenge
To play the traitor. Know, thou wretched thing,
By my command thou wert whipt; and every day
I'll have thee freshly tortured, if thou miss
In the least charge that I impose upon thee.
Though what I speak, for the most part, is true:
Nay, grant thou hadst a thousand witnesses
To be deposed they heard it, 'tis in me
With one word, such is Sforza's confidence
Of my fidelity not to be shaken,
To make all void, and ruin my accusers.
Therefore look to't; bring my wife hotly on
To accuse me to the duke I have an end in't,
Or think what 'tis makes man most miserable,
And that shall fall upon thee. Thou wert a fool
To hope, by being acquainted with my courses,
To curb and awe me; or that I should live
Thy slave, as thou didst saucily divine:
For prying in my counsels, still live mine.

[Exit.

GRACCHO
I am caught on both sides. This 'tis for a puisne

In policy's Protean school, to try conclusions
With one that hath commenced, and gone out doctor.
If I discover what but now he bragg'd of,
I shall not be believed: if I fall off
From him, his threats and actions go together,
And there's no hope of safety. Till I get
A plummet that may sound his deepest counsels,
I must obey and serve him: Want of skill
Now makes me play the rogue against my will.

[Exit.

SCENE II. Another Room in the Same

Enter **MARCELIA, TIBERIO, STEPHANO** and **GENTLEWOMAN.**

MARCELIA
Command me from his sight, and with such scorn
As he would rate his slave!

TIBERIO
'Twas in his fury.

STEPHANO
And he repents it, madam.

MARCELIA
Was I born
To observe his humours! or, because he dotes,
Must I run mad?

TIBERIO
If that your Excellence
Would please but to receive a feeling knowledge
Of what he suffers, and how deep the least
Unkindness wounds from you, you would excuse
His hasty language.

STEPHANO
He hath paid the forfeit
Of his offence, I'm sure, with such a sorrow,
As, if it had been greater, would deserve
A full remission.

MARCELIA
Why, perhaps, he hath it;

And I stand more afflicted for his absence,
Than he can be for mine: so, pray you, tell him.
But, till I have digested some sad thoughts,
And reconciled passions that are at war
Within myself, I purpose to be private:
And have you care, unless it be Francisco,
That no man be admitted.

[Exit **GENTLEWOMAN**.

TIBERIO
How! Francisco?

'STEPHANO
He, that at every stage keeps livery mistresses;
The stallion of the state!

TIBERIO
They are things above us,
And so no way concern us.

STEPHANO
If I were
The duke, (I freely must confess my weakness,)

[Enter **FRANCISCO**.

I should wear yellow breeches; Here he comes.

TIBERIO
Nay, spare your labour, lady, we know our duty,
And quit the room.

STEPHANO
Is this her privacy!
Though with the hazard of a check, perhaps,
This may go to the duke.

[Exeunt **TIBERIO** and **STEPHANO**.

MARCELIA
Your face is full
Of fears and doubts: the reason?

FRANCISCO
O, best madam,
They are not counterfeit. I, your poor convert,
That only wish to live in sad repentance,

To mourn my desperate attempt of you,
That have no ends nor aims, but that your goodness
Might be a witness of my penitence,
Which seen, would teach you how to love your mercy
Am robb'd of that last hope. The duke, the duke,
I more than fear, hath found that I am guilty.

MARCELIA
By my unspotted honour, not from me;
Nor have I with him changed one syllable,
Since his return, but what you heard.

FRANCISCO
Yet malice
Is eagle eyed, and would see that which is not;
And jealousy's too apt to build upon
Unsure foundations.

MARCELIA
Jealousy!

FRANCISCO [Aside]
It takes.

MARCELIA
Who dares but only think I can be tainted?
But for him, though almost on certain proof,
To give it hearing, not belief, deserves
My hate for ever.

FRANCISCO
Whether grounded on
Your noble, yet chaste favours shewn unto me;
Or her imprisonment, for her contempt
To you, by my command, my frantic wife
Hath put it in his head.

MARCELIA
Have I then lived
So long, now to be doubted? Are my favours
The themes of her discourse? or what I do,
That never trod in a suspected path,
Subject to base construction? Be undaunted;
For now, as of a creature that is mine,
I rise up your protectress: all the grace
I hitherto have done you, was bestow'd
With a shut hand; it shall be now more free,
Open, and liberal. But let it not,

Though counterfeited to the life, teach you
To nourish saucy hopes.

FRANCISCO
May I be blasted,
When I prove such a monster!

MARCELIA
I will stand then
Between you and all danger. He shall know,
Suspicion overturns what confidence builds;
And he that dares but doubt when there's no ground,
Is neither to himself nor others sound.

[Exit.

FRANCISCO
So, let it work! Her goodness, that denied
My service, branded with the name of lust,
Shall now destroy itself; and she shall find,
When he's a suitor, that brings cunning arm'd
With power, to be his advocates, the denial
Is a disease as killing as the plague,
And chastity a clue that leads to death.
Hold but thy nature, duke, and be but rash
And violent enough, and then at leisure
Repent; I care not.
And let my plots produce this long'd for birth,
In my revenge I have my heaven on earth.

[Exit.

SCENE III. Another Room in the Same

Enter **SFORZA**, **PESCARA**, and **THREE GENTLEMEN**.

PESCARA
You promised to be merry.

1ST GENTLEMAN
There are pleasures,
And of all kinds, to entertain the time.

2ND GENTLEMAN
Your excellence vouchsafing to make choice
Of that which best affects you.

SFORZA

Hold your prating.
Learn manners too; you are rude.

3RD GENTLEMAN

I have my answer,
Before I ask the question. [Aside.

PESCARA

I must borrow
The privilege of a friend, and will; or else
Iam like these, a sen-ant, or, what's worse,
A parasite to the sorrow Sforza worships
In spite of reason.

SFORZA

Pray you, use your freedom;
And so far, if you please, allow me mine,
To hear you only; not to be compell'd
To take your moral potions. I am a man,
And, though philosophy, your mistress, rage for't,
Now I have cause to grieve I must be sad;
And I dare shew it.

PESCARA

Would it were bestow'd
Upon a worthier subject!

SFORZA

Take heed, friend.
You rub a sore, whose pain will make me mad;
And I shall then forget myself and you.
Lance it no further.

PESCARA

Have you stood the shock
Of thousand enemies, and outfaced the anger
Of a great emperor, that vow'd your ruin,
Though by a desperate, a glorious way,
That had no precedent? are you return 'd with honour,
Loved by your subjects? does your fortune court you,
Or rather say, your courage does command it?
Have you given proof, to this hour of your life,
Prosperity, that searches the best temper,
Could never puff you up, nor adverse fate
Deject your valour? Shall, I say, these virtues,
So many and so various trials of

Your constant mind, be buried in the frown
(To please you, I will say so) of a fair woman?
Yet I have seen her equals.

SFORZA
Good Pescara,
This language in another were profane;
In you it is unmannerly. Her equal!
I tell you as a friend, and tell you plainly,
(To all men else my sword should make reply,)
Her goodness does disdain comparison,
And, but herself, admits no parallel.
But you will say she's cross; 'tis fit she should be,
When I am foolish; for she's wise, Pescara,
And knows how far she may dispose her bounties,
Her honour safe; or, if she were averse,
'Twas a prevention of a greater sin
Ready to fall upon me; for she's not ignorant,
But truly understands how much I love her,
And that her rare parts do deserve all honour.
Her excellence increasing with her years too,
I might have fallen into idolatry,
And, from the admiration of her worth,
Been taught to think there is no Power above her;
And yet I do believe, had angels sexes,
The most would be such women, and assume
No other shape, when they were to appear
In their full glory.

PESCARA
Well, sir, I'll not cross you,
Nor labour to diminish your esteem,
Hereafter, of her. 'Since your happiness
As you will have it; has alone dependence
Upon her favour, from my soul I wish you
A fair atonement.

SFORZA
Time, and my submission,

[Enter **TIBERIO** and **STEPHANO**.

May work her to it. O! you are well return 'd;
Say, am I blest? hath she vouchsafed to hear you?
Is there hope left that she may be appeased?
Let her propound, and gladly I'll subscribe
To her conditions.

TIBERIO
She, sir, yet is froward,
And desires respite, and some privacy.

STEPHANO
She was harsh at first; but, ere we parted, seem'd not
Implacable.

SFORZA
There's comfort yet: I'll ply her
Each hour with new ambassadors of more honours,
Titles, and eminence: my second self,
Francisco, shall solicit her.

STEPHANO
That a wise man,
And what is more, a prince that may command,
Should sue thus poorly, and treat with his wife,
As she were a victorious enemy,
At whose proud feet, himself, his state, and country,
Basely begg'd mercy!

SFORZA
What is that you mutter?
I'll have thy thoughts.

STEPHANO
You shall. You are too fond,
And feed a pride that's swollen too big already,
And surfeits with observance.

SFORZA
O my patience!
My vassal speak thus?

STEPHANO
Let my head answer it,
If I offend. She, that you think a saint,
I fear, may play the devil.

PESCARA
Well said, old fellow. [Aside.

STEPHANO
And he that hath so long engross'd your favours,
Though to be named with reverence, lord
Francisco,
Who, as you purpose, shall solicit for you,

I think's too near her.

[**SFORZA** lays his hand on his sword.

PESCARA
Hold, sir! this is madness.

STEPHANO
It may be they confer of joining lordships;
I'm sure he's private with her.

SFORZA
Let me go,
I scorn to touch him; he deserves my pity,
And not my anger. Dotard! and to be one
Is thy protection, else thou durst not think
That love to my Marcelia hath left room
In my full heart for any jealous thought:
That idle passion dwell with thick-skinn'd tradesmen,
The undeserving lord, or the unable!
Lock up thy own wife, fool, that must take physic
From her young doctor, physic upon her back,
Because thou hast the palsy in that
That makes her active, r I could smile to think
What wretched things they are that dare be jealous ,
Were I match 'd to another Messaline,
While I found merit in myself to please her,
I should believe her chas'te, and would not seek
To find out my own torment; but, alas!
Enjoying one that, but to me, 's a Dian,
I am too secure.

TIBERIO
This is a confidence
Beyond example.

[Enter **GRACCHO**, **ISABELLA**, and **MARIANA**.

GRACCHO
There he is now speak,
Or be for ever silent.

SFORZA
If you come
To bring me comfort, say that you have made
My peace with my Marcelia.

ISABELLA

I had rather
Wait on you to your funeral.

SFORZA
You are my mother;
Or, by her life, you were dead else.

MARIANA
Would you were,
To your dishonour! and, since dotage makes you
Wilfully blind, borrow of me my eyes,
Or some part of my spirit. Are you all flesh?
A lump of patience only? no fire in you?
But do your pleasure: here your mother was
Committed by your sen-ant, (for I scorn
To call him husband,) and myself, your sister,
If that you dare remember such a name,
Mew'd up, to make the way open and free
For the adultress, I am unwilling
To say, a part of Sforza.

SFORZA
Take her head off!
She hath blasphemed, and by our law must die!

ISABELLA
Blasphemed! for calling of a whore,
a whore?

SFORZA
O hell, what do I suffer!

MARIANA
Or is it treason
For me, that am a subject, to endeavour
To save the honour of the duke, and that
He should not be a wittol on re
For by posterity 'twill be believed,
As certainly as now it can be proved,
Francisco, the great minion, that sways all,
To meet the chaste embraces of the dutchess,
Hath leap'd into her bed.

SFORZA
Some proof, vile creature!
Or thou hast spoke thy last.

MARIANA

The public fame,
Their hourly private meetings; and, e'en now,
When, under a pretence of grief or anger,
You are denied the joys due to a husband,
And made a stranger to her, at all times
The door stands open to him; To a Dutch
This were enough, but to a right Italian
A hundred thousand witnesses.

ISABELLA
Would you have us
To be her bawds?

SFORZA
O the malice
And envy of base women, that, with horror,
Knowing their own defects and inward guilt,
Dare lie, and swear, and damn, for what's most false,
To cast aspersions upon one untainted!
Ye are in your natures devils, and your ends,
Knowing your reputation sunk for ever,
And not to be recover'd, to have all
Wear your black livery. Wretches! you have raised
A monumental trophy to her pureness,
Returns upon yourselves; and, if my love
Could suffer an addiction, I'm so far
From giving credit to you, this would teach me
More to admire and serve her. You are not worthy
To fall as sacrifices to appease her;
And therefore live till your own envy burst you.

ISABELLA
All is in vain; he is not to be moved.

MARIANA
She has bewitch'd him.

PESCARA
Tis so past belief,
To me it shews a fable.

[Enter **FRANCISCO**, speaking to a **SERVANT** within.

FRANCISCO
On thy life,
Provide my horses, and without the port
With care attend me.

SERVANT [within]
I shall, my lord.

GRACCHO
He's come.
What gimcrack have we next?

FRANCISCO
Great sir.

SFORZA
Francisco,
Though all the joys in women are fled from me,
In thee I do embrace the full delight
That I can hope from man.

FRANCISCO
I would impart,
Please you to lend your ear, a weighty secret,
I am in labour to deliver to you.

SFORZA
All leave the room.

[Exeunt **ISABELLA**, **MARIANA** and **GRACCHO**.

Excuse me, good Pescara,
Ere long I will wait on you.

PESCARA
You speak, sir,
The language I should use.

[Exit.

SFORZA
Be within call,
Perhaps we may have use of you.

TIBERIO
We shall, sir.

[Exeunt **TIBERIO** and **STEPHANO**

SFORZA
Say on, my comiort.

FRANCISCO

Comfort! no, your torment,
For so my fate appoints me. I could curse
The hour that gave me being.

SFORZA
What new monsters
Of misery stand ready to devour me?
Let them at once dispatch me.

FRANCISCO
Draw your sword then,
And, as you wish your own peace, quickly kill me;
Consider not, but do it.

SFORZA
Art thou mad?

FRANCISCO
Or, if to take my life be too much mercy,
As death, indeed, concludes all human sorrows,
Cut off my nose and ears; pull out an eye,
The other only left to lend me light
To see my own deformities. Why was I born
Without some mulct imposed on me by nature?
Would from my youth a loathsome leprosy
Had run upon this face, or that my breath
Had been infectious, and so made me shunn'd
Of all societies! Curs'd be he that taught me
Discourse or manners, or lent any grace
That makes the owner pleasing in the eye
Of wanton women! since those parts, which others
Value as blessings, are to me afflictions,
Such my condition is.

SFORZA
I am on the rack:
Dissolve this doubtful riddle.

FRANCISCO
That I alone,
Of all mankind, that stand most bound to love you,
And study your content, should be appointed,
Not by my will, but forced by cruel fate,
To be your greatest enemy! not to hold you
In this amazement longer, in a word,
Your dutchess loves me.

SFORZA

Loves thee!

FRANCISCO
Is mad for me,
Pursues me hourly.

SFORZA
Oh!

FRANCISCO
And from hence grew
Her late neglect of you.

SFORZA
O women! women!

FRANCISCO
I labour'd to divert her by persuasion,
Then urged your much love to her, and the danger;
Denied her, and with scorn.

SFORZA
'Twas like thyself.

FRANCISCO
But when I saw her smile, then heard her say,
Your love and extreme dotage, as a cloak,
Should cover our embraces, and your power
Fright others from suspicion; and all favours
That should preserve her in her innocence,
By lust inverted to be used as bawds;
I could not but in duty (though I know
That the relation kills in you all hope
Of peace hereafter, and in me 'twill shew
Both base and poor to rise up her accuser)
Freely discover it.

SFORZA
Eternal plagues
Pursue and overtake her! for her sake,
To all posterity may he prove a cuckold,
And, like to me, a thing so miserable
As words may not express him, that gives trust
To all-deceiving women! Or, since it is
The will of heaven, to preserve mankind,
That we mijst know and couple with these serpents,
No wise man ever, taught by my example,
Hereafter use his wife with more respect

Than he would do his horse that does him service;
Base woman being in her creation made
A slave to man.,. But, like a village nurse,
Stand I now cursing and considering, when
The tamest fool would do! Within there!
Stephano,
Tiberio, and the rest! I will be sudden,
And she shall know and feel, love in extremes
Abused, knows no degree in hate.

[Enter **TIBERIO** and **STEPHANO**.

TIBERIO
My lord.

SFORZA
Go to the chamber of that wicked woman

STEPHANO
What wicked woman, sir?

SFORZA
The devil, my wife.
Force a rude entry, and, if she refuse
To follow you, drag her hither by the hair,
And know no pity; any gentle usage
To her will call on cruelty from me,
To such as shew it. Stand you staring? Go,
And put my will in act.

STEPHANO
There's no disputing.

TIBERIO
But 'tis a tempest, on the sudden raised,
Who durst have dream'd of?

[Exeunt **TIBERIO** and **STEPHANO**.

SFORZA
Nay, since she dares damnation,
I'll be a fury to her.

FRANCISCO
Yet, great sir,
Exceed not in your fury; she's yet guilty
Only in her intent.

SFORZA
Intent, Francisco!
It does include all fact; and I might sooner
Be won to pardon treason to my crown,
Or one that kill'd my father.

FRANCISCO
You are wise,
And know what's best to do: yet, if you please,
To prove her temper to the height, say only
That I am dead, and then observe how far
She'll be transported. I'll remove a little,
But be within your call. Now to the upshot!
Howe'er, I'll shift for one.

[Aside and exit.

[Re-enter **TIBERIO**, **STEPHANO**, and **GUARD** with **MARCELIA**.

MARCELIA
Where is this monster,
This walking tree of jealousy, this dreamer,
This horned beast that would be?
Oh! Are you here, sir?
Is it by your commandment or allowance,
I am thus basely used? "Which of my virtues,
My labours, services, and cares to plea you,
For, to a man suspicious and unthankful,
Without a blush I may be mine own trumpet
Invites this barbarous course? dare you look on me
Without a seal of shame?

SFORZA
Impudence,
How ugly thou appear 'st now! Thy intent
To be a whore, leaves thee not blood enough
To make an honest blush: what had the act done?

MARCELIA
Return'd thee the dishonour thou deserv'st;
Though willingly I had given up myself
To every common letcher.

SFORZA
Your chief minion,
Your chosen favourite, your woo'd Francisco,
Has dearly paid for't; for, wretch! know, he's dead,
And by my hand.

MARCELIA
The bloodier villain thou
But 'tis not to be wonder 'd at, thy love
Does know no other object: thou hast kill'd then,
A man I do profess I loved; a man
For whom a thousand queens might well be rivals.
But he, I speak it to thy teeth, that dares be
A jealous fool, dares be a murderer,
And knows no end in mischief.

SFORZA
I begin now
In this my justice.

[Stabs her.

MARCELIA
'Oh! I have fool'd myself
Into my grave, and only grieve for that
Which, when you know you've slain an innocent,
You needs must suffer.

SFORZA
An innocent! Let one
Call in Francisco; for he lives, vile creature,

[Exit **STEPHANO**.

To justify thy falsehood, and how often,
With whorish flatteries, thou hast tempted him;
I being only fit to live a stale,
A bawd and property to your wantonness.

[Re-enter **STEPHANO**.

STEPHANO
Signior Francisco, sir, but even now
Took horse without the ports.

MARCELIA
We are both abused,
And both by him undone. Stay, death, a little,
Till I have clear'd me to my lord, and then
I willingly obey thee. O, my Sforza!
Francisco was not tempted, but the tempter;
And, as he thought to win me, shew'd the warrant
That you sign'd for my death.

SFORZA
Then I believe thee;
Believe thee innocent too.

MARCELIA
But, being contemn 'd.
Upon his knees with tears he did beseech me,
Not to reveal it; I, soft-hearted fool,
Judging his penitence true, was won unto it:
Indeed, the unkindness to be sentenced by you,
Before that I was guilty in a thought,
Mademe put on a seeming anger towards you,
And now behold the issue! As I do,
May heaven forgive you!

[Dies.

TIBERIO
Her sweet soul has left
Her beauteous prison.

STEPHANO
Look to the duke; he stands
As if he wanted motion.

TIBERIO
Grief hath stopp'd he organ of his speech.

STEPHANO
Take up this body,
And call for his physicians.

SFORZA
O, my heart-strings!

[Exeunt.

ACT V

SCENE I. The Milanese. A Room in Eugenia's House

Enter **FRANCISCO** and **EUGENIA** in male attire.

FRANCISCO
Why, could'st thou think, Eugenia, that rewards.

Graces, or favours, though strew'd thick upon me,
Could ever bribe me to forget mine honour?
Or that I tamely would sit down, before
I had dried these eyes still wet with showers of tears,
By the fire of my revenge? look up, my dearest!
For that proud fair, that, thief-like, stepp'd between
Thy promis'd hopes, and robb'd thee of a fortune
Almost in thy possession, hath found,
With horrid proof, his love, she thought her glory,
And an assurance of all happiness,
But hastened her sad ruin.

EUGENIA
Do not flatter
A grief that is beneath it; for, however
The credulous duke to me proved false and cruel,
It is impossible he could be wrought
To look on her, but with the eyes of dotage,
And so to serve her.

FRANCISCO
Such, indeed, I grant,
The stream of his affection was, and ran
A constant course, till I, with cunning malice
And yet I wrong my act, for it was justice,
Made it turn backwards; and hate, in extremes,
(Love banish 'd from his heart,) to fill the room:
In a word, know the fair Marcelia's dead.

EUGENIA
Dead!

FRANCISCO
And by Sforza 's hand. Does it not move you?
How coldly you receive it! I expected
The mere relation of so great a blessing,
Borne proudly on the wings of sweet revenge.
Would have call'd on a sacrifice of thanks,
And joy not to be bounded or conceal 'd.
You entertain it with a look, as if
You wish'd it were undone.

EUGENIA
Indeed I do:
For, if my sorrows could receive addition,
Her sad fate would increase, not lessen them.
She never injured me, but entertain'd
A fortune humbly offer'd to her hand,

Which a wise lady gladly would have kneel'd for.
Unless you would impute it as a crime,
She was' more fair than I, and had discretion
Not to deliver up her virgin fort,
Though strait besieged with flatteries, vows, and tears,
Until the church had made it safe and lawful.
And had I been the mistress of her judgment
And constant temper, skilful in the knowledge
Of man's malicious falsehood, I had never,
Upon his hell-deep oaths to marry me,
Given up my fair name, and my maiden honour,
To his foul lust; nor lived now, being branded
In the forehead for his whore, the scorn and shame
Of all good women.

FRANCISCO
Have you then no gall,
Anger, or spleen, familiar to your sex?
Or is it possible, that you could see
Another to possess what was your due,
And not grow pale with envy?

EUGENIA
Yes, of him
That did deceive me. There's no passion, that
A maid so injured ever could partake of,
But I have dearly suffer'd. These three years,
In my desire and labour of revenge,
Trusted to you, I have endured the throes
Of teeming women; and will hazard all
B'ate can inflict on me, but I will reach
Thy heart, false Sforza! You have trifled with me,
And not proceeded with that fiery zeal,
I look'd for from a brother of your spirit.
Sorrow forsake me, and all signs of grief
Farewell for ever! Vengeance, arm'd with fury,
Possess me wholly now!

FRANCISCO
The reason, sister,
Of this strange metamorphosis?

EUGENIA
Ask thy fears:
Thy base, unmanly fears, thy poor delays,
Thy dull forgetfulness equal with death;
My wrong, else, and the scandal which can never
Be wash'd off from our house, but in his blood,

Would have stirr'd up a coward to a deed
In which, though he had fallen, the brave intent
Had crown'd itself with a fair monument
Of noble resolution. In this shape
I hope to get access; and, then, with shame,
Hearing my sudden execution, judge
What honour thou hast lost, in being transcended
By a weak woman.,

FRANCISCO
Still mine own, and dearer!
And yet in this you but pour oil on fire,
And offer your assistance where it needs not,
And, that you may perceive I lay not fallow,
But had your wrongs stamp'd deeply on my heart
By the iron pen of vengeance, I attempted,
By whoring her, to cuckold him: that failing,
I did begin his tragedy in her death,
To which it served as prologue, and will make
A memorable story of your fortunes
In my assured revenge: Only, best sister,
Let us not lose ourselves in the performance,
By your rash undertaking: we will be
As sudden as you could wish.

EUGENIA
Upon those terms
I yield myself and cause to be disposed of
As you think fit.

[Enter a **SERVANT**.

FRANCISCO
Thy purpose?

SERVANT
There's one Graccho,
That follow'd you, it seems, upon the track,
Since you left Milan, that's Importunate
To have access, and will not be denied:
His haste, he says, concerns you.

FRANCISCO
Bring him to me. [Exit Servant.
Though he hath laid an ambush for my life,
Or apprehension, yet I will prevent him,
And work mine own ends out.

[Enter **GRACCHO**.

GRACCHO
Now for my whipping!
And if I now outstrip him not, and catch him,
And by a new and strange way too, hereafter
I'll swear there are worms in my brains. [Aside]

FRANCISCO
Now, my good Graccho!
We meet as 't were by miracle.

GRACCHO
Love, and duty,
And vigilance in me for my lord's safety,
First taught me to imagine you were here,
And then to follow you. All's come forth, my lord,
That you could wish conceal'd. The dutchess' wound,
In the duke's rage put home, yet gave her leave
To acquaint him with your practices, which your flight
Did easily confirm.

FRANCISCO
This I expected;
But sure you come provided of good counsel,
To help in my extremes.

GRACCHO
I would not hurt you.

FRANCISCO
How! hurt me? such another word 's thy death;
Why, dar'st thou think it can fall in thy will,
To outlive what I determine?

GRACCHO [Aside]
How he awes me!

FRANCISCO
Be brief; what brought thee hither?

GRACCHO
Care to inform you
You are a condemn'd man, pursued and sought for,
And your head rated at ten thousand ducats
To him that brings it.

FRANCISCO

Very good.

GRACCHO
All passages
Are intercepted, and choice troops of horse
Scour o'er the neighbour plains; your picture sent
To every state confederate with Milan:
That, though I grieve to speak it, in my judgment,
So thick your dangers meet, and run upon you,
It is impossible you should escape
Their curious search.

EUGENIA
Why, let us then turn Romans,
And, falling by our own hands, mock their threats,
And dreadful preparations.

FRANCISCO
'Twould show nobly;
But that the honour of our full revenge
Were lost in the rash action. No, Eugenia,
Graccho is wise, my friend too, not my servant,
And I dare trust him with my latest secret.
We would, and thou must help us to perform it,
First kill the duke then, fall what can upon us!
For injuries are writ in brass, kind Graccho,
And not to be forgotten.

GRACCHO
He instructs me
What I should do. [Aside.

FRANCISCO
What's that?

GRACCHO
I labour with
A strong desire to assist you with my service;
And now I am deliver 'd of 't.

FRANCISCO
I told you.
Speak, my oraculous Graccho.

GRACCHO
I have heard, sir,
Of men in debt that, lay'd for by their creditors,
In all such places where it could be thought

They would take shelter, chose, for sanctuary,
Their lodgings underneath their creditors' noses,
Or near that prison to which they were design 'd,
If apprehended; confident that there
They never should be sought for.

EUGENIA
Tis a strange one!

FRANCISCO
But what infer you from it?

GRACCHO
This, my lord;
That, since all ways of your escape are stopp'd,
In Milan only, or, what's more, in the court,
Whither it is presumed you dare not come,
Conceal'd in some disguise, you may live safe.

FRANCISCO
And not to be discover'd?

GRACCHO
But by myself.

FRANCISCO
By thee! Alas! I know thee honest,
Graccho,
And I will put thy counsel into act,
And suddenly. Yet, not to be ungrateful
For all thy loving travail to preserve me,
What bloody end soe'er my stars appoint,
Thou shalt be safe, good Graccho. Who's within there?

GRACCHO
In the devil's name, what means he?

[Enter **SERVANTS**.

FRANCISCO
Take my friend
Into your custody, and bind him fast:
I would not part with him.

GRACCHO
My good lord.

FRANCISCO

Dispatch:
'Tis for your good, to keep you honest,
Graccho!
I would not have ten thousand ducats tempt you,
Being of a soft and wax -like disposition.
To play the traitor; nor a foolish itch
To be revenged for your late excellent whipping.
Give you the opportunity to offer
My head for satisfaction. Why, thou fool!
I can look through and through thee; thy intents
Appear to me as written in thy forehead,
In plain and easy characters: and but that
I scorn a slave's base blood should rust that sword
That from a prince expects a scarlet dye,
Thou now wert dead; but live, only to pray
For good success to crown my undertakings';
And then, at my return, perhaps, I'll free thee,
To make me further sport. Away with him!
I will not hear a syllable.

[Exeunt **SERVANTS** with **GRACCHO**.

We must trust
Ourselves, Eugenia; and though we make use of
The counsel of our servants, that oil spent,
Like snuffs that do offend, we tread them out.
But now to our last scene, which we'll so carry,
That few shall understand how 'twas begun,
Till all, with half an eye, may see 'tis done.

[Exeunt.

SCENE II. Milan. A Room in the Castle

Enter **PESCARA**, **TIBERIO**, and **STEPHANO**.

PESCARA
The like was never read of.

STEPHANO
In my judgment,
To all that shall but hear it, 'twill appear
A most impossible fable.

TIBERIO
For Francisco,

My wonder is the less, because there are
Too many precedents of unthankful men
Raised up to greatness, which have after studied
The ruin of their makers.

STEPHANO
But that melancholy,
Though ending in distraction, should work
So far upon a man, as to compel him
To court a thing that has nor sense nor being,
Is unto me a miracle.

PESCARA
'Troth, I'll tell you,
And briefly as I can, by what degrees
He fell into this madness. When, by the care
Of his physicians, he was brought to life,
As he had only pass'd a fearful dream,
And had not acted what I grieve to think on,
He call'd for fair Marcelia, and being told
That she was dead, he broke forth in extremes,
(I would not say blasphemed,) and cried that heaven,
For all the offences that mankind could do,
Would never be so cruel as to rob it
Of so much sweetness, and of so much goodness;
That not alone was sacred in herself,
But did preserve all others innocent,
That had but converse with her.) Then it came
Into his fancy that she was accused
By his mother and his sister; thrice he curs'd them,
And thrice his desperate hand was on his sword
T' have kill'd them both; but he restrain'd, and they
Shunning his fury, spite of all prevention
He would have turned his rage upon himself;
When wisely his physicians, looking on
The dutchess' wound, to stay his ready hand,
Cried out, it was not mortal.

TIBERIO
'Twas well thought on.

PESCARA
He easily believing what he wish'd,
More than a perpetuity of pleasure
In any object else; flatier'd by hope,
Forge'tting his own greatness, he fell prostrate
At the doctors' feet, implored their aid, and swore,
Provided they recover'd her, he would live

A private man, and they should share his dukedom.
They seem'd to promise fair, and every hour
Vary their judgments, as they find his fit
To suffer intermission or extremes:
For his behaviour since

SFORZA [within]
As you have pity
Support her gently.

PESCARA
Now, be your own witnesses;
I am prevented.

[Enter **SFORZA, ISABELLA, MARIANA, DOCTORS,** and **SERVANTS** with the body of **MARCELIA.**

SFORZA
Carefully, I beseech you,
The gentlest touch torments her; and then think
What I shall suffer. O you earthly gods,
You second natures, that from your great master,
Who join'd the limbs of torn Hippolitus,
And drew upon himself the Thunderer's envy,
Are taught those hidden secrets that restore
To life death-wounded men! you have a patient,
On whom to express the excellence of art,
Will bind even heaven your debtor, though it pleases
To make your hands the organs of a work
The saints will smile to look on, and good angels
Clap their celestial wings to give it plaudits.
How pale and wan she looks! O pardon me,
That I presume (dyed o'er with bloody guilt.
Which makes me, I confess, far, far unworthy)
To touch this snow-white hand. How cold it is!
This once was Cupid's fire-brand, and still
'Tis so to me. How slow her pulses beat too
Yet in this temper, she is all perfection,
And mistress of a heat so full of sweetness,
The blood of virgins, in their pride of youth,
Are balls of snow or ice compared unto her.

MARIANA
Is not this strange?

ISABELLA
Oh! cross him not, dear daughter;
Our conscience tells us we have been abused,
Wrought to accuse the innocent, and with him

Are guilty of a fact

[Enter a **SERVANT**, and whispers **PESCARA**.

MARIANA
'Tis now past help.

PESCARA
With me? What is he?

SERVANT
He has a strange aspect;
A Jew by birth, and a physician
By his profession, as he says, who, hearing
Of the duke's frenzy, on the forfeit of
His life will undertake to render him
Perfect in every part: provided that
Your lordship's favour gain him free access.
And your power with the duke a safe protection,
Till the great work be ended.

PESCARA
Bring me to him;
As I find cause, I'll do.

[Exeunt **PESCARA** and **SERVANT**

SFORZA
How sound she sleeps!
Heaven keep her from a lethargy! How long
(But answer me with comfort, I beseech you)
Does your sure judgment tell you that these lids,
That cover richer jewels than themselves,
Like envious night, will bar these glorious suns
From shining on me?

1ST DOCTOR
We have given her, sir,
A sleepy potion, that will hold her long,
That she may be less sensible of the torment
Her searching of her wound will put her to.

2ND DOCTOR
She now feels little; but, if we should wake her,
To hear her speak would fright both us and you,
And therefore dare not hasten it.

SFORZA

I am patient.
You see I do not rage, but wait your pleasure.
What do you think she dreams of now? for sure,
Although her body's organs are bound fast,
Her fancy cannot slumber.

1ST DOCTOR
That, sir, looks on
Your sorrow for your late rash act, with pity
'Of what you suffer for it, and prepares
To meet the free confession of your guilt
With a glad pardon.

SFORZA
She was ever kind;
And her displeasure, though call'd on, shortlived
Upon the least submission. O you Powers,
That can convey our thoughts to one another
Without the aid of eyes or ears, assist me!
Let her behold me in a pleasing dream

[Kneels.

'Thus, on my knees before her; (yet that duty
In me is not sufficient;) let her see me
Compel my mother, from whom I took life,
And this my sister, partner of my being,
To bow thus low unto her; let her hear us
In my acknowledgment freely confess
That we in a degree as high are guilty
As she is innocent. Bite your tongues, vile creatures,
And let your inward horror fright your souls,
For having belied that pureness to come near which,
All women that posterity can bring forth
Must be, though striving to be good, poor rivals.
And for that dog Francisco, that seduced me,
In wounding her, to rase a temple built
To chastity and sweetness, let her know
I'll follow him to hell, but I will find him,
And there live a fourth fury to torment him.
Then, for this curs'd hand and arm that guided
The wicked steel, I'll have them, joint by joint,
With burning irons sear'd off, which I will eat,
I being a vulture fit to taste such carrion;
Lastly

1ST DOCTOR
You are too loud, sir; you disturb

Her sweet repose.

SFORZA
I am hush'd. Yet give us leave,
Thus prostrate at her feet, our eyes bent downwards,
Unworthy, and ashamed, to look upon her,
To expect her gracious sentence.

2ND DOCTOR
He's past hope.

1ST DOCTOR
The body too will putrify, and then
We can no longer cover the imposture.

TIBERIO
Which, in his death, will quickly be discover'd.
I can but weep his fortune.

STEPHANO
Yet be careful
You lose no minute to preserve him; time
May lessen his distraction.

[Re-enter **PESCARA**, with **FRANCISCO**, as a Jew doctor, and **EUGENIA** disguised as before.

FRANCISCO
I am no god, sir,
To give a new life to her; yet I'll hazard
My head, I'll work the senseless trunk t 'appear
To him as it had got a second being,
Or that the soul, that's fled from't, were call'd back
To govern it again. I will preserve it
In the first sweetness, and by a strange vapour,
Which I'll infuse into her mouth, create
A seeming breath; I'll make her veins run high too,
As if they had true motion.

PESCARA
Do but this,
Till we use means to win upon his passions
T'endure to hear she's dead with some small patience,
And make thy own reward.

FRANCISCO
The art I use
Admits no looker on: I only ask
The fourth part of an hour, to perfect that

I boldly undertake.

PESCARA
I will procure it.

2ND DOCTOR
What stranger's this?

PESCARA
Sooth me in all I say;
There's a main end in it.

FRANCISCO
Beware!

EUGENIA
I am warn'd.

PESCARA
Look up, sir, cheerfully; comfort in me
Flows strongly to you.

SFORZA
From whence came that sound?
Was it from my Marcelia? If it were,

[Rises.

I rise, and joy will give me wings to meet it.

PESCARA
Nor shall your expectation be deferr'd
But a few minutes. Your physicians are
Mere voice, and no performance; I have found
A man that can do wonders. Do not hinder
The dutchess wish'd recovery, to enquire
Or what he is, or to give thanks, but leave him
To work this miracle.

SFORZA
Sure, 'tis my good angel.
I do obey in all things: be it death
For any to disturb him, or come near,
Till he be pleased to call us. O, be prosperous,
And make a duke thy bondman!

[Exeunt all but **FRANCISCO** and **EUGENIA**.

FRANCISCO
'Tis my purpose;
If that to fall a long-wish'd sacrifice
To my revenge can be a benefit.
I'll first make fast the doors; so!

EUGENIA
You amaze me:
What follows now?

FRANCISCO
A full conclusion
Of all thy wishes. Look on this, Eugenia,
Even such a thing, the proudest fair on earth
(For whose delight the elements are ransack'd,
And art with nature studied to preserve her,)
Must be, when she is summon'd to appear
In the court of Death. But I lose time.

EUGENIA
What mean you?

FRANCISCO
Disturb me not. Your ladyship looks pale;
But I, your doctor, have a ceruse for you.
See, my Eugenia, how many faces,
That are adorned in court, borrow these helps,

[Paints the cheeks.

And pass for excellence, when the better part
Of them are like to this. Your mouth smells sour too,
But here is that shall take away the scent;
A precious antidote old ladies use,
When they would kiss, knowing their gums are rotten.

[Paints the lips.

These hands, too, that disdained to take a touch
From any lip, whose owner writ not lord,
Are now but as the coarsest earth; but I
Am at the charge, my bill not to be paid too,
To give them seeming beauty.

[Paints the hands.

So! 'tis done.
How do you like my workmanship?

EUGENIA
I tremble:
And thus to tyrannize upon the dead,
Is most inhuman.

FRANCISCO
Come we for revenge,
And can we think on pity! Now to the upshot,
And, as it proves, applaud it. My lord the duke!
Enter with joy, and see the sudden change
Your servant's hand hath wrought.

[Re-enter **SFORZA** and the rest.

SFORZA
I live again
In my full confidence that Marcelia may
Pronounce my pardon. Can she speak yet?

FRANCISCO
No:
You must not look for all your joys at once;
That will ask longer time.

PESCARA
Tis wondrous strange!

SFORZA
By all the dues of love I have had from her,
This hand seems as it was when first I kiss'd it.
These lips invite too: I could ever feed
Upon these roses, they still keep their colour
And native sweetness: only the nectar's wanting,
That, like the morning dew in flowery May,
Preserved them in their beauty.

[Enter **GRACCHO** hastily.

GRACCHO
Treason, treason!

TIBERIO
Gallup the guard.

FRANCISCO
Graccho! then we are lost.

[Enter **GUARD**.

GRACCHO
I am got off, sir Jew; a bribe hath done it,
For all your serious charge; there's no disguise
Can keep you from my knowledge.

SFORZA
Speak.

GRACCHO
I am out of breath,
But this is

FRANCISCO
Spare thy labour, fool, Francisco.

ALL
Monster of men!

FRANCISCO
Give me all attributes
Of all you can imagine, yet I glory
To be the thing I was born. I AM Francisco;
Francisco, that was raised by you, and made
The minion of the time; the same Francisco,
That would have whored this trunk, when it had life;
And, after, breathed a jealousy upon thee,
As killing as those damps that belch out plagues
When the foundation of the earth is shaken:
I made thee do a deed heaven will not pardon,
Which was to kill an innocent.

SFORZA
Call forth the tortures
For all that flesh can feel.

FRANCISCO
I dare the worst.
Only, to yield some reason to the world
Why I pursued this course, look on this face,
Made old by thy base falsehood: 'tis Eugenia.

SFORZA
Eugenia!

FRANCISCO
Does it start you, sir? my sister,

Seduced and fool'd by' thee: but thou must pay
The forfeit of thy falsehood. Does it not work yet!
Whate'er becomes of me, which I esteem not,
THOU art mark'd for the grave: I've given thee poison
In this cup, now observe me, which, thy lust
Carousing deeply of, made thee forget
Thy vow'd faith to Eugenia.

PESCARA
O damn'd villain!

ISABELLA
How do you, sir?

SFORZA
Like one
That learns to know in death what punishment
Waits on the breach of faith. Oh! now I feel
An Ætna in my entrails. I have lived
A prince, and my last breath shall be command.
I burn, I burn! yet ere life be consumed.
Let me pronounce upon this wretch all torture
That witty cruelty can invent.

PESCARA
Away with him!

TIBERIO
In all things we will serve you.

FRANCISCO
Farewell, sister!
Now I have kept my word, torments I scorn:
I leave the world with glory. They are men,
And leave behind them name and memory,
That, wrong'd, do right themselves before they die.

[Exeunt **GUARD** with **FRANCISCO**.

STEPHANO
A desperate wretch!

SFORZA
I come: Death! I obey thee.
Yet I will not die raging; for, alas!
My whole life was a frenzy. Good Eugenia,
In death forgive me. As you love me, bear her
To some religious house, there let her spend

The remnant of her life: when I am ashes,
Perhaps she'll be appeased, and spare a prayer
For my poor soul. Bury me with Marcelia,
And let our epitaph be

[Dies.

TIBERIO
His speech is stopp'd.

STEPHANO
Already dead!

PESCARA
It is in vain to labour
To call him back. We'll give him funeral,
And then determine of the state affairs:
And learn, from this example, There's no trust
In a foundation that is built on lust.

[Exeunt.

PHILIP MASSINGER – A SHORT BIOGRAPHY

This biography was initially written in 1830

Very few materials exist for a life of Massinger beyond the entries of the Parish Register or the College Books, and a few slender intimations scattered here and there in the dedications to his plays. From these scanty sources the following brief memoir is derived.

Our author was born at Salisbury in the year 1584: he was the son of Arthur Massinger, a gentleman in the service of Henry, the second Earl of Pembroke. We must not suppose, from his being thus attached to the family of a nobleman, that the father of our poet was a person of inferior birth and station. In those days the word servant carried with it no sense of degradation. The great lords and officers of the court numbered inferior nobles among their followers. We read, in Cavendish's Life of Wolsey, that "my Lord Percy, the son and heir of the Earl of Northumberland, attended upon and was servitor to the lord-cardinal:" and from the situation which Arthur Massinger held in the household of so high and influential a person as the Earl of Pembroke, we might be justly led to argue rather favourably than unfavourably of his family and his connexions. "There were," says Mr. Gifford, "many considerations which united to render this state of dependance respectable and even honourable. The secretaries, clerks, and assistants, of various departments, were not then, as now, nominated by the government, but left to the choice of the person who held the employment; and as no particular dwelling was officially set apart for their residence, they were entertained in the house of their principal. That communication, too, between noblemen of power and trust, both of a public and private nature, which is now committed to the post, was in those days managed by confidential servants, who were despatched from one to the other, and even to the sovereign;" and, indeed, the father of our poet himself was, we know, in one instance thus employed as the bearer of communications from his patron to Elizabeth. We read in The Sidney Letters, "Mr. Massinger is newly come up from the Earl of Pembroke with letters to the queen for his lordship's leave to be away this St. George's Day." This was an errand which would not have been intrusted to the execution of any inconsiderable person: unimportant as the occasion may appear to us, it would not have been regarded in that light by Elizabeth; for no monarch ever exacted from the nobility, and particularly from her officers of state, a more rigid and scrupulous compliance with stated order than this princess.

With regard to the early youth of Massinger, we possess no information whatever. Mr. Gifford supposes that it might have been passed at Wilton, a seat belonging to the Earl of Pembroke, in the neighbourhood of Salisbury; but this mode of disposing of his early years rests on a very improbable conjecture. It may occasionally have happened that the child of a favourite dependant was admitted as the companion of the younger branches of the patron's family, and allowed to receive his education among them; but this was certainly not an ordinary case; and, like Cavendish, a large majority of the great man's servants and dependants "left wife and children, home and family, rest and quietness, only to serve him."—Massinger was most likely educated at the grammar-school of Salisbury, where many distinguished characters have received the rudiments of their education, among whom the elegant and accomplished Addison is to be numbered. But wherever the first years of our poet's life may have been spent, and whatever may have been the nature of his education, we know that at the age of eighteen (May 14, 1602) he was entered at the university of Oxford, and became a commoner of St. Alban's Hall.

Massinger resided at Oxford about four years, and then abruptly left it, without taking any degree. The cause of this sudden departure is ascribed by Mr. Gifford to the death of his father, from whom his supplies were derived: but Davies relates a very different story, and asserts that the Earl of Pembroke, who had sent him to the university and maintained him there, withdrew the necessary allowance in consequence of his having misapplied the time demanded for severer studies, in the pursuit of a more attractive but less profitable description of literature. Each opinion is equally ungrounded on the basis of any substantial evidence, and rests almost entirely on the imagination of the biographer: what slight authority there is favours the latter supposition, which, perhaps, on the whole, is most consistent with the known circumstances of the case. Anthony Wood, who was born, lived, and died at Oxford; who spent his time in collecting and recording the gossip which circulated in the university respecting the characters and conduct of its more distinguished sons; and whose evidence, however indifferent it may be, is the best that can be obtained upon the subject, confirms the representation of Davies:— "Massinger," says Wood, "gave his mind more to poetry and romance, for about four years or more, than to logic and philosophy, which he ought to have done, as he was patronised to that end." This passage corroborates the account of Davies so far as to intimate that patronage was afforded to our author, and that cause of dissatisfaction was given to the patron; but it goes no farther: it does not even state to whom the poet was indebted for assistance, nor that the misapplication of his academic hours was at all resented by the friend from whom the assistance was received: but still Wood is very probably correct in his information that other than his paternal funds were depended upon for maintaining Massinger at the university; and if such was the case, there can be no question from whose hands they must have proceeded; while the simple fact of his having been totally neglected, from the time of his father's death, by the whole of the Pembroke family, till after the demise of the earl, carries with it a strong suspicion that some offence was committed on the side of the poet, and tenaciously remembered on the side of the peer. Henry, the second Earl of Pembroke, died (1601) the year before Massinger was admitted at Oxford; and William, the third earl, to whom the father of Massinger continued attached during life, is universally and justly considered one of the brightest ornaments of the courts of Elizabeth and James. He was a man of generous and liberal disposition; the distinguished patron of arts and learning; and a lover of poetry, which he himself cultivated with some degree of success. It is not probable—it is impossible—that such a man should have allowed the highly talented son of an old and faithful servant of his family to be checked in his course of study, and abandoned to maintain, through the early years of life, a single-handed contest with adversity, for the want of that pecuniary aid which he could have yielded and never missed, unless some strong and decided cause of displeasure had existed. Had Massinger been merely forced to leave the university, as Mr. Gifford supposes, because the funds necessary to maintain him there had failed with the life of his father, we impute an act of illiberality to the Earl of Pembroke which is inconsistent with the whole tenor of his life and character. From whatever source the expenses of our author's education were originally defrayed, their suddenly ceasing argues in favour of the account intimated by Wood and detailed by Davies. If his father had, during his life, supported him at the university, there must have been some reason for the earl's not continuing that support when the father of Massinger was no more; and perhaps the most honourable supposition for both parties is that which represents the earl as offended by the bent of our author's studies and pursuits. By adopting this view of the case we are saved from the painful necessity of either assuming, on the one hand, that a nobleman distinguished among the most amiable characters of his age allowed a highly gifted and meritorious young man, a natural dependant of his house, to languish in the want of that countenance and protection on which he had an hereditary claim; or, on the other hand, that Massinger had incurred the displeasure of his natural and hereditary patron by the commission of some more crying offence.

Every, even the slightest, surmise of Mr. Gifford is deserving attention and respect; but I cannot admit the supposition by which he would account for the alienation that subsisted between the Earl of Pembroke and our author. That distinguished critic has inferred, from the religious sentiments contained in The Virgin Martyr, that Massinger was a Roman catholic, and for that cause neglected by the protector of his father. But if the intimations scattered through this play and others should be received as sufficient evidence of the faith of Massinger, we must, on similar evidence—the intimations contained in Measure for Measure, for instance—conclude that the religion of Shakspeare was the same; and then we are cast back upon our old difficulty, and have to explain why William Earl of Pembroke, a celebrated patron of literary men, and of dramatists in particular, scorned to yield his notice to the catholic Massinger, while (to use the expression of Heminge and Condell) he "prosequuted" the catholic Shakspeare and "his works with so much favour?" There are many reasons for believing Shakspeare to have been a member of the church of Rome; and the patronage afforded him by the Earl of Pembroke proves, that that nobleman extended his liberality to men of genius without any regard to distinctions of faith; but, on the other hand, we have no just grounds for assuming that Massinger really did hold the same opinions. The only evidence we have upon this point, that afforded by the general tone of his writings, is of a most vague and superficial description. What, in fact, can be inferred from it? We may from such a source derive very satisfactory information respecting the sentiments which would be favourably received by the audience, but very little respecting those of the author. The truth is, that though the national religion was reformed in its liturgy and articles, the feelings, prejudices, and superstitions of the people were still almost entirely catholic; and Massinger, like any other dramatic author, writing for the amusement of the people, necessarily addressed them in a language they would understand, and with sentiments that accorded with their own. Besides, as a poet, he would never carry his theological distinctions to his literary labours: Voltaire himself is catholic in his tragedies; and Massinger naturally adopted the creed which was most suitable to the purposes of poetry, and afforded the most picturesque ceremonies and romantic situations. I feel inclined, therefore, to dismiss entirely the theory suggested by Mr. Gifford, for these two reasons; first, supposing our author to have been a catholic, we have no reason for condemning the Earl of Pembroke as a bigot and a persecutor, who would close his eyes to the merits of so great an author, because his faith did not tally with his own; and, secondly, we have no sufficient grounds for supposing him to have been a catholic at all. But with regard to all such visionary conjectures, thinking is literally a waste of thought.

Whatever may have been the nature of Massinger's studies at Oxford, it is quite certain, from the general character of his works, that his time could not have been wasted there; and his literary acquirements, at the period of his leaving the university, appear to have been multifarious and extensive. He was about two-and-twenty (1606) when he arrived in London, where, as he more than once observes, he was driven by his necessities, and somewhat inclined, perhaps, by the peculiar bent of his talents, to dedicate himself to the service of the stage.

The theatre, when Massinger first took up his abode in the metropolis, must have presented attractions of all others the most calculated to excite the interest, and inspire the imagination, of a young man of sensibility, taste, and education like our poet. No art ever attained a more rapid maturity than the dramatic art in England. The people had, indeed, been long accustomed to a species of exhibition, called MIRACLES or MYSTERIES, founded on sacred subjects, and performed by the ministers of religion themselves, on the holy festivals, in or near the churches, and designed to instruct the ignorant in the leading facts of sacred history. From the occasional introduction of allegorical characters, such as Faith, Death, Hope, or Sin, into these religious dramas, representations of another kind, called MORALITIES, had by degrees arisen, of which the plots were more artificial, regular, and connected, and which were entirely formed of such personifications: but the first rough draught of a regular tragedy and comedy— Lord Sackville's Gorboduc, and Still's Gammer Gurton's Needle—were not produced till within the latter half of the sixteenth century, and little more than twenty years before the stage acquired its highest splendour in the productions of Shakspeare.

About the end of the sixteenth century, the attention of the public began to be more generally directed to the drama; and it throve most admirably beneath the cheering beams of popular favour. The theatrical performances which in the early part of Elizabeth's reign had been exhibited on temporary stages, erected in such halls or apartments as the actors could procure, or, more generally, in the yards of the larger inns, while the spectators surveyed them from the surrounding windows and galleries, began to find more convenient and permanent habitations. About the year 1569, a regular playhouse, under the appropriate name of The Theatre, was erected. It is supposed to have stood somewhere in Blackfriars; and, three years after the commencement of this establishment, the queen, yielding to her own inclination for such amusements, and disregarding the remonstrances of the Puritans, granted licence and authority to the servants of the Earl of Leicester ("for the recreation of her loving subjects, as for her own solace and pleasure when she should think good to see them") to exercise their occupation throughout the whole realm of England. From this time the number of theatres increased with the increasing demands of the people. Various noblemen had their respective companies of performers, who were associated as their servants, and acted under their protection; and when Massinger left Oxford, and commenced dramatic author, there were no less than seven principal theatres open in the metropolis.

With respect to the interior arrangements, there were very few points of difference between our modern theatres and those of the days of Massinger. The prices of admission, indeed, were considerably cheaper: to the boxes the entrance was a shilling; to the pit and galleries only sixpence. Sixpence also was the price paid for stools upon the stage; and these seats, as we learn from Decker's Gull's Hornbook, were particularly affected by the wits and critics of the time. The conduct of the audience was less restrained by the sense of public decorum, and smoking tobacco, playing at cards, eating and drinking, were generally prevalent among them. The hours of performance were also earlier: the play commencing at one o'clock. During the representation a flag was unfurled at the top of the theatre; and the stage, according to the universal practice of the age, was strewn with rushes; but, in all other respects, the theatres of Elizabeth and James's days seem to have borne a perfect resemblance to our own. They had their pit, where the inferior class of spectators, the groundlings, vented their clamorous censure or approbation; they had their boxes—rooms as they were called—to which the right of exclusive admission was engaged by the night, for the more affluent portion of the audience; and there were again the galleries, or scaffoldings above the boxes, for those who were content to purchase less commodious situations at a cheaper rate. On the stage, in the same manner, the appointments appear to have been nearly of the same description as at present. The curtain divided the audience from the actors, which, at the third sounding, not indeed of the bell, but of the trumpet, was drawn for the commencement of the performance. Malone, in his account of the ancient theatre, supposes that there were no moveable scenes; that a permanent elevation of about nine feet was raised at the back of the stage, from which, in many of the old plays, part of the dialogue was spoken; and that there was a private box on each side this platform. Such an arrangement would have destroyed all theatrical illusion; and it seems extraordinary that any spectators should desire to fix themselves in a station where they could have seen nothing but the backs and trains of the performers; but, as Malone himself acknowledges the spot to have been inconvenient, and that "it is not very easy to ascertain the precise situation where these boxes really were", it may very reasonably be presumed, that they were not placed in the position that the historian of the English stage has supposed. As to the permanent floor, or upper stage, of which he speaks, he may or may not be correct in his statement. All that his quotations upon the subject really establish is, that in the old, as in the modern theatre, when the actor was to speak from a window, or balcony, or the walls of a fortress, the requisite ingenuity was not wanting to contrive a representation of the place. But with regard to the use of painted moveable scenery, it is not possible, from the very circumstances of the case, to believe him correct in his theory. Such a contrivance could not have escaped our ancestors. All the materials were ready to their hands. They had not to invent for themselves, but merely to adapt an old invention to that peculiar purpose; and at a time when every better-furnished apartment was adorned with tapestry; when even the rooms of the commonest taverns were hung with painted cloths; while all the materials were constantly before their eyes, we can hardly believe our forefathers to have been so deficient in ingenuity, as to have missed the simple contrivance of converting the common ornaments of their walls into the decorations of their theatres. But, in fact, the use of scenery was almost co-existent with the introduction of dramatic representations in this country. In the Chester Mysteries (1268), the most ancient and complete collection of the kind which we possess, is found the following stage direction: "Then Noe shall go into the arke with all his familye, his wife excepte. The arke must be boarded round about; and upon the boardes all the beastes and fowles, hereafter rehearsed, must be painted, that their wordes may agree with their pictures." In this passage we have a clear reference to a painted scene. It is not likely that, in the lapse of three centuries, while all other arts were in a state of rapid improvement, and the art of dramatic writing, perhaps, more rapidly and successfully improved than any other, the art of theatrical decoration should have alone stood still. It is not improbable that their scenes were few; and that they were varied, as occasion might require, by the introduction of different pieces of stage furniture. Mr. Gifford, who adheres to the opinions of Malone, says, "A table with a pen and ink thrust in, signified that the stage was a counting-house; if these were withdrawn and two stools put in their place, it was then a tavern." And this might be perfectly satisfactory as long as the business of the play was supposed to be passing within doors; but when it was removed to the open air, such meagre devices would no longer be sufficient to guide the imagination of the audience, and some new method must have been adopted to indicate the place of action. After giving the subject very considerable attention, I cannot help thinking that Steevens was right in rejecting Malone's theory, and concluding that the spectators were, as at the present day, assisted in following the progress of the story by means of painted moveable scenery. This opinion is confirmed by the ancient stage directions. In the folio Shakspeare, 1623, we read "Enter Brutus in his orchard; Enter Timon in the woods; Enter Timon from the cave." In Coriolanus, "Marcius follows them to the gates and is shut in." Innumerable instances of the same kind might be cited to prove that the ancient stage was not so defective in the necessary decorations as some antiquaries of great authority would represent. "It may be added," says Steevens, "that the dialogue of our old dramatists has such perpetual reference to objects supposed visible to the audience, that the want of scenery could not have failed to render many of the descriptions absurd. Banquo examines the outside of Inverness castle with such minuteness, that he distinguishes even the nests which the martens had built under the projecting part of its roof. Romeo, standing in a garden, points to the tops of fruit-trees gilded by the moon. The prologue speaker to the second part of Henry the Fourth expressly shows the spectators 'This worm-eaten hold of ragged stone,' in which Northumberland was lodged. Iachimo takes the most exact inventory of every article in Imogen's bed-chamber, from the silk and silver of which her tapestry was wrought, down to the Cupids that support her andirons. Had not the inside of the apartment, with its proper furniture, been represented, how ridiculous must the action of Iachimo have appeared! He must have stood looking out of the room for the particulars supposed to be visible within it." The works of Massinger would afford innumerable instances of a similar kind to vindicate the opinion which Steevens has asserted on the testimony of Shakspeare alone. But on this subject there is one passage which appears to me quite conclusive. Must not all the humour of the mock play in The Midsummer Night's Dream have been entirely lost, unless the audience before whom it was performed were accustomed to all the embellishments requisite to give effect to a dramatic representation, and could consequently estimate the absurdity of those shallow contrivances and mean substitutes for scenery devised by the ignorance of the clowns?

In only one respect do I perceive any material difference between the mode of representation at the time of Massinger and at present: in his day, the female parts were performed by boys. This custom, which must in many cases have materially injured the illusion of the scene, was in others of considerable advantage: it furnished the stage with a succession of youths, regularly educated for the art, to fill, in every department of the drama, the characters suited to their age. When the lad had become too tall for Juliet, he had acquired the skill, and was most admirably fitted, both in age and appearance, for performing the part which Garrick considered the most difficult on the stage, because it needed "an old head upon young shoulders," the ardent and arduous character of Romeo. When the voice had "the mannish crack," that rendered the youth unfit to appear as the representative of the gentle Imogen, the stage possessed in him the very person that was wanting to do justice to the princely sentiments of Arviragus or Guiderius.

Such was the state of the stage when Massinger arrived in the metropolis, and dedicated his talents to its service. He joined a splendid fraternity, for Shakspeare, Jonson, Beaumont, Fletcher, Shirley, were then flourishing at the height of their reputation, and the full vigour of their genius. Massinger came among them no unworthy competitor for such honours and emoluments as the theatre could afford. Of the honours, indeed, he seems to have reaped a very fair and equitable portion; of the emoluments, the harvest was less abundant. In those days, very little pecuniary reward was to be gained by the dramatic poet, unless, as indeed was most frequently the case, he added the profession of the actor to that of the author, and recited the verses which he wrote. The distinguished performers of that time, Alleyn, Burbage, Heminge, Condell, Shakspeare, all appear to have died in independent, if not affluent, circumstances; but the remuneration obtained by the poet was most miserably curtailed. The price given at the theatre for a new play fluctuated between ten and twenty pounds; the copyright, if the piece was printed, might produce from six to ten pounds more; in addition to these sums, the dedication-fee may be reckoned, the usual amount of which was forty shillings. Our author appears to have produced about two or three plays every year. Most of them were successful; but, even with this industry and good fortune, his annual income would rarely have exceeded fifty pounds: and we cannot, therefore, feel surprised at finding him continually speaking of his necessities; or that the only existing document connected with his life should be one that represents him in a state of pecuniary embarrassment.

Among the papers of Dulwich College, the indefatigable Mr. Malone discovered the following letter tripartite, which, coming from persons of such deserved celebrity, cannot fail of interesting the reader.

"To our most loving friend, Mr. Phillip Hinchlow, esquire, these.

"Mr. Hinchlow,

"You understand our unfortunate extremitie, and I doe not thincke you so void of Christianitie but that you would throw so much money into the Thames as wee request now of you, rather than endanger so many innocent lives. You know there is xl. more, at least, to be receaved of you for the play. We desire you to lend us vl. of that, which shall be allowed to you; without which, we cannot be bayled, nor I play any more till this be dispatch'd. It will lose you xxl. ere the end of the next weeke, besides the hindrance of the next new play. Pray, sir, consider our cases with humanity, and now give us cause to acknowledge you our true freind in time of neede. Wee have entreated Mr. Davison to deliver this note, as well to witness your love as our promises, and alwayes acknowledgement to be ever

"Your most thankfull and loving friends,
"NAT. FIELD."

"The money shall be abated out of the money remayns for the play of Mr. Fletcher and ours.
"ROB. DABORNE."

"I have ever found you a true loving friend to mee, and in soe small a suite, it beinge honest, I hope you will not fail us.
"PHILIP MASSINGER."

Indorsed.
"Received by mee, Robert Davison, of Mr. Hinchlow, for the use of Mr. Daboerne, Mr. Feeld, Mr. Messenger, the sum of vl.
"ROB. DAVISON."

The occasion of the distress in which these three distinguished persons were involved it is not possible to fathom. We may imagine a thousand emergencies, either creditable or discreditable to the fame of the writers, with which the letter would perfectly tally; but, on such slight and vague intimations, no ingenuity could determine which was most likely to be correct. But from the document a circumstance is ascertained, which, before its discovery, had been called in question. Sir Aston Cockayne, a friend of Massinger, had asserted in a volume of poems, published in 1658, that our author had written in conjunction with Fletcher; Davies doubted this report, but the above letter establishes the fact beyond the possibility of dispute.

Massinger is known to have produced thirty-seven plays for the stage, a list of which is given at the conclusion of this memoir. Sixteen entire plays and the fragment of another, The Parliament of Love, alone are extant. No less than eleven of his productions, in manuscript, were in possession of Mr. Warburton (Somerset Herald), and destroyed with the rest of that gentleman's invaluable collection by his cook, who, ignorant of their worth, used them as waste paper for the purposes of the kitchen.

The great and various merits of the works of Massinger will be better seen in the following volumes than in any elaborate, critical dissertation. If our author be compared with the other dramatic writers of his age, we cannot long hesitate where to place him. More natural in his characters and more poetical in his diction than Jonson or Cartwright, more elevated and nervous than Fletcher, the only writers who can be supposed to contest his pre-eminence, Massinger ranks immediately under Shakspeare himself. Our poet excels, perhaps, more in the description than in the expression of passion; this may in some measure be ascribed to his attention to the fable: while his scenes are managed with consummate skill, the lighter shades of character and sentiment are lost in the tendency of each part to the catastrophe. The melody, force, and variety of his versification are always remarkable. The prevailing beauties of his productions are dignity and elegance; their predominant fault is want of passion.

Massinger's last play—which is unfortunately lost—The Anchoress of Pausilippo, was acted Jan. 26, 1640, about six weeks before his death, which happened on the 17th of March, 1640. He went to bed in good health, says Langbaine, and was found dead in the morning, in his own house on the Bankside. He was buried in the churchyard of St. Saviour's, and the comedians paid the last sad duty to his name, by attending him to the grave.

It does not appear, though every stone and every fragment of a stone has been carefully examined, that any monument or inscription of any kind marked the place where his dust was deposited. "The memorial of his mortality," says Gifford, "is given with a pathetic brevity, which accords but too well with the obscure and humble passages of his life: March 20, 1639-40, buried Philip Massinger, A STRANGER."

Such is all the information that remains to us of this distinguished poet. But though we are ignorant of every circumstance respecting him but that he lived, wrote, and died, we may yet form some idea of his personal character from the recommendatory poems prefixed to his several plays, in which, as Mr. Gifford justly observes, the language of his panegyrists, though warm, expresses an attachment apparently derived not so much from his talents as his virtues: he is their beloved, much-esteemed, dear, worthy, deserving, honoured, long-known, and long-loved friend. All the writers of his life represent him as a man of singular modesty, gentleness, candour, and affability; nor does it appear that he ever made or found an enemy.

PHILIP MASSINGER – A CONCISE BIBLIOGRAPHY

As would be expected many works from this time no longer exist either in part or their entirety. Further many playwrights collaborated on plays or revised them for later performances and we have used the latest position known on each of them for the bibliography below.

Solo Plays
The Maid of Honour, tragicomedy (c. 1621; printed 1632)

The Duke of Milan, tragedy (c. 1621–3; printed 1623, 1638)
The Unnatural Combat, tragedy (c. 1621–6; printed 1639)
The Bondman, tragicomedy (licensed 3 December 1623; printed 1624)
The Renegado, tragicomedy (licensed 17 April 1624; printed 1630)
The Parliament of Love, comedy (licensed 3 November 1624; MS)
A New Way to Pay Old Debts, comedy (c. 1625; printed 1632)
The Roman Actor, tragedy (licensed 11 October 1626; printed 1629)
The Great Duke of Florence, tragicomedy (licensed 5 July 1627; printed 1636)
The Picture, tragicomedy (licensed 8 June 1629; printed 1630)
The Emperor of the East, tragicomedy (licensed 11 March 1631; printed 1632)
Believe as You List, tragedy (rejected by the censor in January, but licensed 6 May 1631; MS)
The City Madam, comedy (licensed 25 May 1632; printed 1658)
The Guardian, comedy (licensed 31 October 1633; printed 1655)
The Bashful Lover, tragicomedy (licensed 9 May 1636; printed 1655)

Collaborations with John Fletcher
Sir John van Olden Barnavelt, tragedy (August 1619; MS)
The Little French Lawyer, comedy (c. 1619–23; printed 1647)
A Very Woman, tragicomedy (c. 1619–22; licensed 6 June 1634; printed 1655)
The Custom of the Country, comedy (c. 1619–23; printed 1647)
The Double Marriage, tragedy (c. 1619–23; Printed 1647)
The False One, history (c. 1619–23; printed 1647)
The Prophetess, tragicomedy (licensed 14 May 1622; printed 1647)
The Sea Voyage, comedy (licensed 22 June 1622; printed 1647)
The Spanish Curate, comedy (licensed 24 October 1622; printed 1647)
The Lovers' Progress or The Wandering Lovers, tragicomedy (licensed Dec 1623; rev 1634; printed 1647)
The Elder Brother, comedy (c. 1625; printed 1637).

Collaborations with John Fletcher and Francis Beaumont
Thierry and Theodoret, tragedy (c. 1607; printed 1621)
The Coxcomb, comedy (1608–10; printed 1647)
Beggars' Bush, comedy (c. 1612–15; revised 1622; printed 1647)
Love's Cure, comedy (c. 1612–15; revised 1625; printed 1647).

Collaborations with John Fletcher and Nathan Field
The Honest Man's Fortune, tragicomedy (1613; printed 1647)
The Queen of Corinth, tragicomedy (c. 1616–18; printed 1647)
The Knight of Malta, tragicomedy (c. 1619; printed 1647).

Collaborations with Nathan Field
The Fatal Dowry, tragedy (c. 1619, printed 1632); adapted by Nicholas Rowe: The Fair Penitent

Collaborations with John Fletcher, John Ford, and William Rowley, or John Webster
The Fair Maid of the Inn, comedy (licensed 22 January 1626; printed 1647).

Collaborations with John Fletcher, Ben Jonson, and George Chapman
Rollo Duke of Normandy, or The Bloody Brother, tragedy (c. 1616–24; printed 1639).

Collaborations with Thomas Dekker
The Virgin Martyr, tragedy (licensed 6 October 1620; printed 1622).

Collaborations with Thomas Middleton and William Rowley
The Old Law, comedy (c. 1615–18; printed 1656).

www.ingramcontent.com/pod-product-compliance
Lightning Source LLC
Chambersburg PA
CBHW060121050426
42448CB00010B/1987